John Bishop
June 1987

Courage
to Live

Courage
to Live

JOHN BISHOP

Judson Press, Valley Forge

COURAGE TO LIVE

Copyright © 1976
Judson Press, Valley Forge, PA 19481

All rights reserved. No part of this publication may be reproduced, stored in a retrieval system, or transmitted in any form or by any means, electronic, mechanical, photocopying, recording, or otherwise, without the prior permission of the copyright owner, except for brief quotations included in a review of the book.

Translations of the Bible quoted in this volume are as follows:

The Holy Bible, King James Version.

The Holy Bible, the Revised Standard Version of the Bible, copyrighted 1952 and 1971 by the Division of Christian Education of the National Council of the Churches of Christ in the United States of America. Used by permission.

The Bible: A New Translation by James Moffatt. Copyright 1954 by James Moffatt. By permission of Harper & Row, Publishers, Inc.

Library of Congress Cataloging in Publication Data
Bishop, John, 1908-
  Courage to live.

  Includes bibliographical references.
  1. Christian life—Methodist author. I.   Title.
BV4501.2.B53   248'.48'7   76-999
ISBN 0-8170-0697-4

Printed in the U.S.A. ⊕

TO MY WIFE
in gratitude for her constant encouragement and help

Introduction

The basic human need is not for money or material things but for courage to live, to win the victory of the spirit. People today are frightened and anxious. They find the burdens of living too much for them, and when some crisis arises, then the bottom drops out of their lives. The gospel of Jesus Christ promises the peace of God which passes all understanding—not only inner tranquillity but also the resources we need to live the victorious life.

At the close of my active ministry of forty-two years serving the Methodist Church in Britain and the United States I would like to tell of problems Christ has helped persons to overcome and to call upon my experience as a pastor in dealing with people in all kinds of need. It has been said: "Everybody has a problem or is a problem or lives with one." Wherever there are problems, there are people seeking solutions to them. The problems I have chosen are those which I have met most often in my pastoral work. Every minister who counsels with others knows the questions which, however often a minister seeks to answer them, drain the power and strength out of one. Why is life so unjust? Why do persons suffer? Why could I never realize my heart's desire? Why are there so many complications along the road? Why is life so full of grief and graves?

My experience in the ministry has taught me that there is no problem God and people together cannot solve. There are limitless resources open to everyone through faith in God. But to find those resources, we must go to school with Christ and use the Bible as an unfailing reservoir of spiritual power. Faith in God enables us to stand up against everything that can happen to us, because it gives meaning to life as well as direction and purpose. The person of faith who draws upon the resources of the Christian religion can face the stresses and strains of life without fear of faltering.

The substance of this book was originally given as sermons which met with a most encouraging response. They have been rewritten and enlarged, and my hope is that they may lead those who read them to the help that waits everlastingly beyond all human helps and without which our efforts are futile. I have seen Christ help so many souls at the breaking point to believe in life, to stand upon their feet before God, and to praise him for his grace. If this book can help to touch some lives with the victorious power of Christ, it will not have been written in vain.

John Bishop,
Princeton, New Jersey

Contents

1. The Secret of Overcoming   13
2. The Cure for Care   19
3. How to Face Disappointment   27
4. How to Triumph over Limitations   35
5. How to Master Depression   41
6. Fear—Friend or Foe?   49
7. A Home for the Lonely   57
8. Time—Tyrant or Servant?   65
9. Hindrances to Prayer   71
10. Burdens and How to Bear Them   81
11. The Conquest of Suffering   89
12. God's Word for Eventide   97
13. How to Grieve with Hope   105
14. Looking Death in the Face   113

Notes   121

1

The Secret of Overcoming

"In all these things we are more than conquerors through him that loved us." Romans 8:37

Lloyd C. Douglas wrote a novel some years ago entitled *Green Light* in which the central figure, Dr. Harcourt, the Dean of Trinity Cathedral, is a powerful influence for good in the lives of all the characters. Each one comes to him in a time of need and receives from him the green light signal to go ahead. In his early days as a minister he was a popular preacher for whom a great future was predicted, but through an accident he became permanently crippled. He could not get about without help. At first he was inclined to rebel against this infirmity, but he came to see that a man must stop to learn through suffering before he goes on. So he established a spiritual clinic where sufferers came for help and healing.

One day a doctor comes to the dean in great distress. He thinks of religion as only an opiate, drugging people's senses. While not denying the problems that threaten to overwhelm people, Dr. Harcourt affirms that his trust that the universe is, at its heart,

14 • COURAGE TO LIVE

friendly has sustained him. Even if he is temporarily stopped, ultimately he gets the green light.[1]

The apostle Paul said the same thing as the dean, only in different language. He wrote to the church at Philippi: "Not that I have already obtained this . . . but . . . I press on toward the goal for the prize of the upward call of God in Christ Jesus" (Philippians 3:12, 14, RSV). We sometimes say to those who try to cheer us up in the struggles of life, "You don't know what I'm up against." But Paul does. Look at this list: "Who shall separate us from the love of Christ? shall tribulation, or distress, or persecution, or famine, or nakedness, or peril, or sword?" (Romans 8:35). This covers all the foes that assail the soul. Paul did not have an easy life. He was uncheered by the joys of home and family. He was conscious of his physical defects. He himself said that his bodily presence was weak and his speech contemptible. He suffered from some painful disease which he called a thorn in the flesh. He was absorbed by the cares of all the churches he had founded. He knew the depression caused by failure; yet in spite of persecution and imprisonment his soul never hardened. His joy never grew dim, for he had in himself such great resources that the outward things did not matter very much. His true wealth lay within the storehouse of his soul. Christ was in him, the hope of glory. So he could make this bold claim: "In all these things we are more than conquerors through him that loved us" (Romans 8:37).

Religion is given us to provide us with the means of overcoming. Difficulties are made to be overcome: they are not to be avoided but faced and dealt with. A Scottish minister of the last century lost all his money when the City of Glasgow Bank failed, and this is what he wrote in his diary: "This calamity has been sent to me for some purpose. Difficulties are to meet, to greet, and to beat. Keep your face towards the sun and the shadows will fall behind."[2]

Emergencies have always been necessary for the progress of the race. It was darkness that produced the lamp. It was the fog that caused the invention of the compass. It was winter that clothed men and women, and hunger that drove them to exploration. The aviator can taxi along the ground all day with the wind at his back; but if he hopes to rise, he must drive into the face of the wind. Dr. Fosdick says that there are two kinds of people in the world—those who, like Atlas in the Greek legend, seem to have the world on their back in the sense of having everything on top of them and those who seem to have the world at their feet.

THE SECRET OF OVERCOMING • 15

What meaning can we put to a phrase like this of Paul's—"more than conquerors"? We all have some trouble to meet, perhaps more than one. As Job said, "Man is born unto trouble, as the sparks fly upward" (Job 5:7). Our trouble may be ill-health, a physical handicap, or some misfortune or hardship. Some blow may have fallen on our home or our heart, or it may be just the weary weight of countless little burdens or difficulties from which life gives us no release. What is this victory in which Paul exults?

It is a victory of the spirit in the whole situation. For it is possible to be conqueror but no more. We can, for instance, meet misfortune bravely and not allow it to crush us completely. Sorrow may come and we may not permit it to break our spirit. Business may be very difficult, and yet we may keep a spirit of dogged perseverance that demands real courage. But though we may be conquerors, we may not be more than conquerors. The thing we have to meet may throw a strain upon the spirit in other ways which we cannot bear. How many of the heroic people of history have had some hidden weakness? On the surface all the flags were flying, but behind the scenes there was moral defeat. For trouble often exposes us to self-pity, and by that door all kinds of laxity and self-indulgence may creep in. Hardships out in the world may make us miserable at home. They may put a strain on us which makes us hard to live with. Sorrow may make us resentful, and unconsciously we may vent our secret bitterness upon others. We may let our minds become fretted with anxiety. Worst of all, we may let trouble cloud our faith in God and lose our serenity.

We may let ourselves become so absorbed in our troubles that we have no room for the troubles of others. Misfortune may shut us into a prison even while we take practical steps to deal with it. The needs of others may be forgotten because we are so wrapped up in ourselves. We become self-centered and lonely. We lose sympathy and understanding instead of gaining it. Suffering does not always soften: it sometimes hardens, in which case, even when we are brave about it, we are not completely victorious. This is the great question we have to face: Is the pressure of life thrusting us into unbelief or into the everlasting arms of God? I do not know what God's purpose may be concerning the trial he permits in your life. But I am sure that there is a purpose behind the pressure.

To be more than conquerors means to be victorious in the whole situation. Paul knew that super-victory. He was persecuted, but he never gave way to hatred of those who hurt him. He was faced with all

16 • COURAGE TO LIVE

kinds of misfortune, but he never became resentful nor did he lose his inward peace and joy. The spirit of the New Testament Christians was a joyful serenity, a peace of mind that nothing could destroy. Think of Paul and Silas in prison at Philippi with their feet fast in the stocks; yet at midnight they sang praises to God. That was not only victory but super-victory. It was the overflowing of a life possessed by God at the depths. Has the joy gone out of your life? God wants to bring it back. He wants you to live a life of continual rejoicing. In your experience of his overcoming power you will find a new joy. There was nothing lovely about the crown of thorns which God gave to Christ. There may be nothing lovely about the crown of thorns he has given to you, but it can be transformed into a crown of glory as was Christ's.

The victorious life means even more. Trouble becomes a power for service. Disablement becomes an equipment. Misfortune becomes a means of blessing. It ceases to be an intruder to be overcome and kept from hurting us. Through this victory it becomes a friend. The best example of this was in the life of Christ and most of all in his cross. The most victoriously unselfish thing in history was his prayer for his enemies. It was a miracle amid the absorbing agony for him to think about his enemies at all, much less to care about them. But to use his last breath to pray for their forgiveness was to be more than conqueror.

Our Lord never expected anything but victory. He proclaimed his victory on his last night on earth. On the night in which he was betrayed, he gave thanks and said: "In the world ye shall have tribulation: but be of good cheer; I have overcome the world" (John 16:33). A few hours later they nailed him to a cross. That did not look like victory, but he cried with a loud voice from the cross, "It is finished." That was the shout of a conqueror. It was from that victorious Lord that Paul derived his own certainty of triumph. "In all these things we are more than conquerors through him that loved us" (Romans 8:37). "Thanks be to God, which giveth us the victory through our Lord Jesus Christ" (1 Corinthians 15:57). John had the same assurance, for he wrote, "This is the victory that overcometh the world, even our faith" (1 John 5:4). In the book of Revelation at the close of each message to the seven churches of Asia Minor the risen Lord says: "To him that overcometh I will give" or "He that overcometh shall receive." (See Revelation 2 and 3.) The life of our Lord was the life of a super-conqueror. He overcame the tempter; he

THE SECRET OF OVERCOMING • 17

overcame the powers of evil; he overcame sickness; he overcame the last enemy—death; and ever since, his faithful followers have been more than conquerors through him.

The New Testament does not promise us immunity from suffering or calamity, but it does offer us a confidence in God which no disaster can dispel. Life has been described as a tragedy to those who feel, a comedy to those who think, but a victory to those who believe. As someone has put it: "The greatest Christian faith is like a Rembrandt portrait—an illuminated face shining out of a dark background." A famous painter said, "It's no joke to paint a picture. Into the painting of every picture that is worth anything there comes sometimes this period of despair." No religious faith is won easily. The pearl is only obtained at the price of pain. No enemy, no conflict; no conflict, no victory; no cross, no crown; no rain, no rainbow.

To this same complete victory that Christ won he calls you and me. Perhaps we have never thought that such victory is possible or we may never have seen that things like irritation, anxiety, resentment are a real defeat. But in Christ there is power for victory in the whole situation which trouble brings. It is all in his love for us. He can come down into the prison where we are shut up in fear or resentment and set us free. He can cleanse the hidden chambers of the mind where the fungus of self-pity or anxiety is growing. Have we claimed the completeness of victory? It is this he offers—nothing less. In him we can be more than conquerors.

"For myself," confessed Napoleon, "nature has doomed me to win none but outward victories."[3] But the message of the gospel is that it need not be so with you and me. I do not know what may be the particular problem that is tormenting your soul nor what secret sorrows may be present. I do not know what the future holds for you. I only know that Christ who died for the love of you has given his promise to be with you and to teach you the secret of overcoming. I know that things can never go so far wrong that the living God cannot control and bend them to his will. To know this is to know the victory of the spirit.

When God enters our lives, he comes to reign. He brooks no divided allegiance. When we are mastered by Christ, we achieve the mastery of self. We need not be defeated on the inner battleground of the soul. We can be victors over ourselves and over our circumstances. Even as Christ learned obedience by the things he suffered and pressed on to victory, so may we. He can give us the victory over

18 • COURAGE TO LIVE

the habits which have us in their grip and can enable us by his power to break the chains which bind us, and which by ourselves we are powerless to break. He can give us the victory over the tasks which seem so difficult that they are impossible and teach us that with him all things are possible. He can give us the victory over our fears, our fear of life and our fear of death, so that in his company even the most frightening things lose their terror. He can give us the victory over our temptations and so fill us with his power that no evil things may ever conquer our resistance, and no wrong fascination can ever lure us from his path. He can give us the victory over the faults and weaknesses which continually beset us and overpower us and over the moods by which we are so easily swayed. He can give us the victory over our sorrows, so that even the bitterest sorrow may not take away our joy. He can give us the victory over our handicaps so that out of life, as we know it, whatever it is like, we may yet make a shining thing.

A friend of mine said to me not long ago: "I think I know what Paul had in mind when he said, 'Take unto you the whole armor of God, that ye may be able to withstand in the evil day, and having done all to stand.' When I begin the day with God, I feel like one of the knights of old as he buckled on his armor. If I can take the hard knocks of life a little better than some of my fellows, it is only because I have better resources with which to meet them. I know the truth of the words:

'Who in the strength of Jesus trusts
Is more than conqueror.'"

2

The Cure for Care

"Be careful for nothing; but in every thing by prayer and supplication with thanksgiving let your requests be made known unto God." Philippians 4:6

Care is so common a thing that sooner or later it begins to furrow every face. We are meant to care about many things and to care intensely. If we do not do our daily work with care, we are lazy and dishonest. We must care about details or else ours will be a disordered world. Mothers are anxious about their children: that is no fault; it is natural because of their love for them. The knowledge that a mother does care and that her son's disgrace would strike her like a blow has kept many a lad from doing wrong. The person who takes up a position of responsibility in the church or in the government of the town or country has to care for the welfare of others. Care is one of God's disciplines for fashioning human character.

But this praiseworthy thing may grow into a disease. There is a difference between being careful and being full of care. Our Lord, who knew what was in persons, warned us not to be overanxious. He said, "Do not be anxious about tomorrow" (Matthew 6:34, RSV). He

20 • COURAGE TO LIVE

was not advocating a thoughtless, improvident attitude toward life, but he was forbidding a careworn worry which takes all the joy out of life. He knew that the cares of this world could easily choke the Word. The disease of care is that we forget God's care of us. We care so passionately because no one else seems to care. We grow anxious about the future of our loved ones or about some cause which is dear to our hearts. If we do not care, we say, who will? Living in such a world as this, subject to all the unknown chances of life, how can we help being anxious?

God gave you that sensitive heart, but he also has a heart that cares. Peter advises his converts to cast all their care upon God, for he cares for them. This is how Dr. Moffatt translates his words: "Let all your anxieties fall upon him, for his great interest is in you" (1 Peter 5:7, Moffatt). It has been rightly said that an anxious heart is never a holy heart. Why should we go staggering beneath our load of care when all the time God is by our side, the God who daily bears our burdens? So few of us behave as if we really believed in God. We worry over trifles and lay waste our powers so that when the real crisis comes, we are quite unequal to it. Today we have not finished with yesterday, and we cannot leave tomorrow alone. We have not learned to live a day at a time, believing that as our days, so shall our strength be. We are filled with remorse for the past and fear of the future.

We admit that it is foolish to worry: it never helps but hinders in many ways. Yet we go on worrying. I once asked a friend of mine, "What do you worry about?" Quick as a flash came his reply, "Everything." Anxiety has been called the disease of our age, and my experience bears out the truth of that statement. An American doctor has analyzed the "worriers" who at one time or another have been his patients. Forty percent of them, he found, worried over things which never happened. Thirty percent of the worries related to things in the past which were now beyond their control. Twelve percent were worried about their health, although their only illness was in their imagination. Ten percent worried over their families or their neighbors, though in most cases there was no real ground for their anxiety. Just 8 percent of the worries seemed to have some basis in conditions which needed to be remedied.[1] The Navajo Indians have a phrase for our word "worry"—"my mind is killing me." That exactly describes that useless activity of the mind which keeps thoughts revolving without issuing in action.

What is the remedy? It is no good saying, "Don't worry: it may

THE CURE FOR CARE • 21

never happen" and leave it at that. That old proverb which says, "Never trouble trouble till trouble troubles you," is a bit of homely philosophy that we all need, but it does not go far enough. When real anxiety is upon us, we need something stronger than that on which to stay our souls. Some of us are born worriers; others are not. If we are of a worrying nature, it is no use saying, "What will it all matter a hundred years hence?" What is the good of saying to someone plunged in calamity, "Cheer up, my friend"? Why should he cheer up? We must give him a reason.

Paul, writing out of his own experience, says, "Be careful for nothing; but in every thing by prayer and supplication with thanksgiving let your requests be made known unto God." These words are the soundest and sanest prescription I know against anxiety. They combine religion and psychology. They bid us worry about nothing, pray about everything, and be thankful for anything. "In nothing be anxious"—it begins but it does not end there as the well-meant but futile advice "Don't worry" does. It also does not fall into the error of sympathizing with the anxious person, kindly and welcome though such sympathy is, for the effect of that is to reassure the worrier that such a hard case certainly confirms every reason for anxiety. Paul's advice is sounder. If you tell a person to forget or ignore anxiety, you overlook the fact that the effects of mental repression must be released. Just as an old illness or wound may set up mischief in the system, so a trouble which has caused anxiety may become in itself a minor affair, but real havoc is caused by the state of mind which the trouble stirs up.

We all like to talk about our anxieties—that is the instinct of appeal, the instinct that causes the animal to cry out to its fellows in pain or danger. Paul tells us to take the matter up with God and to go through the whole experience again with him. The alternative to anxiety, the cure for care, is prayer. We are not to forget the things that disturb or frighten us: we are to pray about every one of them, to turn our cares into prayers. "Let your requests be made known unto God." Just tell him; that is enough. His love will understand. His heart needs no persuading.

This advice of the apostle Paul is the counsel of the whole Bible. Text after text seems to say "Don't worry," but it never says that without giving us a reason. If you make a list of all the Scripture passages that tell us not to worry, you will find that God permeates them all. "Cast thy burden upon the Lord, and he shall sustain thee"

22 • COURAGE TO LIVE

(Psalm 55:22). "Commit thy way unto the Lord; trust also in him; and he shall bring it to pass" (Psalm 37:5). "Seek ye first the kingdom of God, and his righteousness; and all these things shall be added unto you" (Matthew 6:33). Put everything into God's hands. The way to be anxious about nothing is to be prayerful about everything.

Paul did not know what a day or an hour might bring forth when he wrote these words to the Philippians. He was a prisoner and at any time he might be put to death for his faith. But no one can detect any gloom or defeatism. In this letter he expresses his joy in Christ. He had the secret of peace and confidence. It was found in the knowledge that his Lord was at hand. Our Lord is always at hand to help, to comfort, and to bless.

The only way to take anxious care out of our hearts and lives is to bring God into them and keep him there. "In every thing." There is nothing too great for God's power and nothing too small for his fatherly care. If a thing is great enough to make me anxious, it is great enough to be spoken about to God. If he is my Friend, then the instinct of friendship will make me tell him everything. If we are not to get help from God by telling him of the little things, there will not be much to speak to him about, for every life is made up of innumerable trifles. We are to speak out all our needs to God. We are not simply to take refuge in his presence. We are to tell him all our worries, share with him all our troubles, and ask for the help that will not be denied.

If we have an anxiety of which we are ashamed to speak to God, that is a sign that we ought not to have it. There are many vague anxieties that oppress us. If we could only define them and put them into words, we would find that we had fancied them a great deal larger than they are. Put your anxieties into definite speech to God and there are very few of them that will survive. Even if we confide our anxieties to an earthly friend, a minister or a doctor, we find that it seems to ease us wonderfully and make our burden lighter. How much more will this be the case if we disclose them to our heavenly Friend!

A university student, bothered by a personal problem, spent an hour with Phillips Brooks, the famous Boston preacher. When he returned to college, a friend asked him, "What did Dr. Brooks say about your problem?" "It did not seem to matter when I talked to Dr. Brooks," was his reply.[2] That should be the effect of prayer, and it will be its effect if we come consciously into the presence of God. John

THE CURE FOR CARE • 23

Wesley was charged with anxious responsibilities that would have reduced most of us to fretful despair, but he never worried because he constantly prayed to God. "I feel and grieve," he said, "but I fret at nothing." If God cares for us, then worry is both unnecessary and irreligious.

How can prayer help us in times of anxiety? It helps us by bringing God himself into our lives. A great deal of worry comes from our leaving God out of the situation. We think of situations in terms of human possibilities and human strength and human wisdom, and if we do that, then there is little wonder that we worry. Prayer marks the end of human wisdom and human effort and leads us to cast ourselves upon our heavenly Father. This method of escape from anxieties has been used by the saints in all ages, and they have found it the way to victory. We read in the story of King Hezekiah about a disturbing and threatening letter which greatly upset him. How did he meet his trouble? He went into the house of the Lord and spread the letter before his God and found relief from anxiety by prayer. (See 2 Kings 19:14-19.) Matthew tells in his Gospel the sad story of the beheading of John the Baptist. It was a tragic blow to the faith of the disciples. What did they do? They went and told the Master. Telling Jesus was the simplest and surest way of escape from the burden of anxiety in those days and it still is today. (See Matthew 14:1-12.)

> O what peace we often forfeit,
> O what needless pain we bear,
> All because we do not carry
> Everything to God in prayer.[3]

Do you believe that everything is in the hands of God, that he is "working his purpose out as year succeeds to year," and that he is calling us to be fellow workers with him in the realization of his purpose? If we had to face tomorrow and its problems unaided and alone, we might well be driven beyond anxiety into despair. But we do not have to stand up to life solitarily and single-handedly. "Lo, I am with you always" is God's promise.

The final piece of advice that the apostle Paul gives is "Be thankful for anything." When he was in prison in Philippi, in the very city to which this letter was written, with his feet fast in the stocks and his back aching from the rod, he and Silas prayed and sang praises to God at midnight. Perhaps it was the recollection of that night which moved him to say to the church there, "by prayer and supplication with thanksgiving let your requests be made known unto God."

24 • COURAGE TO LIVE

In another of his letters Paul says, "Pray without ceasing [and] in every thing give thanks" (1 Thessalonians 5:17-18). It is not the happy people who are thankful; it is the thankful people who are happy. A thankful person has a barricade built against anxiety. Such persons face life with confidence because they are aware of mercy streaming on them from God and from their associates. "All things are for your sakes," says the Apostle, "that the abundant grace might through the thanksgiving of many redound to the glory of God" (2 Corinthians 4:15). "All things" means we must give thanks to God not only for his mercies but also for his trials and tribulations. We must learn to say, "Glory to thee for strength withdrawn, for want and weakness known."

Is it possible to give thanks for every thing? Yes, because the continual remembrance of all that we have known of God's goodness will teach us to be sure, in every change of circumstance and every new event, that this also is part of his mercy. George Matheson, the blind poet-preacher of Scotland, once wrote this prayer: "My God, I have never thanked Thee for my thorn. I have thanked Thee a thousand times for my roses but never once for my thorn. Teach me the glory of my cross; teach me the value of my thorn."[4] That is the highest form of gratitude—when we can give thanks even for our thorn.

To give thanks creates an atmosphere in which anxiety cannot live. It recalls to us causes for gratitude, prayers that have been answered, needs that have been supplied, fears that have proved groundless. It reminds us of past anxieties that have been overcome, and that makes us better able to face the present situation in a hopeful spirit. So in times of stress and strain, when your back is to the wall, recall everything good and pure and worthy of praise.

We must not allow one cloud in the sky to hide from us all the wealth of blue and all the glory of the earth. It is easy for us to allow a fragment of dark to blacken the whole, as a pinhole of light can fog the entire film in a camera. Dr. W. E. Sangster tells of a minister who went to preach in a strange church and was told in the vestry that the front pews were always occupied by the inmates of a home for the blind. He asked one of the officials to inquire whether they would like to choose a hymn they knew. He came back to say that they would like to sing the hymn by Joseph Addison which begins:

> When all Thy mercies, O my God,
> My rising soul surveys,

THE CURE FOR CARE • 25

> Transported with the view, I'm lost
> In wonder, love and praise.

They were blind, but they wanted to sing that last triumphal verse:

> Through all eternity to Thee
> A joyful song I'll raise:
> But oh!, eternity's too short
> To utter all Thy praise.[5]

We can see, and so we should open our eyes widely to the mercies of God and be thankful. There is a familiar hymn which bids us "count your many blessings, name them one by one." It is good but impossible advice. We cannot count all our blessings, for our arithmetic is not good enough. But we can count some of them, and the greatest of all is God's inestimable love in the redemption of the world by our Lord Jesus Christ.

Cast all your anxious care upon God, for he cares for you. That does not mean that we are not required to take care of ourselves. God's care for us is a profound relief, but it is never meant to relieve us of all effort. We are not just to commit everything to God and fold our hands. The only carefree life is the life that is full of care, care for God, care for our fellows, care for ideals. Anxiety is not an evil; it is a schoolmaster to bring us to God.

This is the cure for care—to worry about nothing, to pray about everything, and to be thankful for anything that God allows to come into our lives. Then in place of anxiety there will come a deep peace, "the peace of God, which passeth all understanding, shall keep [guard] your hearts and your minds in Christ Jesus" (Philippians 4:7). The word "guard" suggests a sentinel who challenges all comers and keeps out every foe. So when we are living the life of prayer, the peace of God will stand sentinel at the door of our souls, guarding heart and mind, feelings and thoughts. The way to peace is to take ourselves and all whom we hold dear and place them and ourselves trustingly in prayer into the hands of God. Praise plus Poise plus Prayer equals Perfect Peace. If we learn to turn everything that might be a ground for anxiety into an opportunity for prayer, then we shall find that the promise is true: "Thou wilt keep him in perfect peace, whose mind is stayed on thee: because he trusteth in thee" (Isaiah 26:3).

3

How to Face Disappointment

"Whensoever I take my journey into Spain, I will come to you." Romans 15:24

Deep down in almost every heart you will find a disappointment of some kind. Disappointments may take many forms. They may be mere minor vexations or they may be so crushing and overwhelming that at the time it seems as if there could be no recovery from them. There are disappointments in business, in love, in our friends, or in our children. There are the disappointments which come with age and the inevitable weakening of our powers.

There are disappointments which we bring upon ourselves through an exaggerated self-estimate, which leads us to expect what with better right is given to someone else. There are the disappointments in matters which lie beyond our control that can only be explained as misfortune or bad luck. Can any of us imagine, for example, what it must have meant to Scott and his brave companions in the Antarctic, after incredible toil and hardships, to arrive at the South Pole only to discover that Amundsen had preceded them by a month?

28 • COURAGE TO LIVE

Disappointment is part of the human lot; sooner or later, in one form or another, it overtakes us all. Moreover, it tests us as few things in life do. "Thou, O God," cries one of the psalmists, "hast proved us: thou hast tried us, as silver is tried" (Psalm 66:10). Disappointment is a fire in which everyone's character is tried. There are few sadder things on this earth than disappointed people. They are so cheerless and apt to be bitter, because they have brooded over their disappointments and let them sink into their souls. Since no one can escape disappointment, the important questions for all of us are: how do we react to it? In what spirit do we meet it? What are we making of it? What is it making of us?

Let us turn to the Bible and see what light it sheds on this problem of disappointment. Again and again in the Scriptures we find men wrestling with it. Abraham went out to receive an inheritance, and he died possessing nothing in the Promised Land except a grave. Joseph cherished the dream of a home for his people in Egypt, and the end of his story was a coffin in Egypt. Moses brought the children of Israel out of Egypt, and after forty years of wandering in the desert he stood on Mount Pisgah looking across Jordan to the Canaan of his dreams, the land flowing with milk and honey. To his bitter disappointment he was told that his people would enter it but not under his leadership. David wanted to build a house worthy of God, but his vision was never to become a reality for him. He died with his purpose unfulfilled.

Paul was on his second missionary journey, and he and his companion, Silas, planned to launch a campaign in Bithynia, on the shores of the Black Sea. Luke tells us in the Acts, "They attempted to go into Bithynia, but the Spirit of Jesus did not allow them; so, passing by Mysia, they went down to Troas. And a vision appeared to Paul in the night: a man of Macedonia was standing beseeching him and saying, 'Come over to Macedonia and help us.' And when he had seen the vision, immediately we sought to go on into Macedonia, concluding that God had called us to preach the gospel to them" (Acts 16:7-10, RSV). So Christianity passed over from Asia into Europe. Paul was checkmated, but he won the game. He was thwarted, and it led him to his crown. Eager to advance with the good news, there arose before him the divine "No thoroughfare." Yet that hour when he was hindered so was the hour when God was honoring him and leading him to a mighty service of God of which he had never dreamed.

HOW TO FACE DISAPPOINTMENT • 29

Later in his life Paul was disappointed again. One of his dreams was to travel to Spain where, at the edge of the then known world, he might preach the gospel. On his return he hoped to have fellowship with the Christians in Rome. "Whensoever I take my journey into Spain," he wrote to them, "I will come to you" (Romans 15:24). But he never got to Spain and only entered Rome as a prisoner.

Our Lord had many disappointments. There was the rich young ruler whom he loved and who was unable to muster enough courage to follow him. There was Philip who wanted absolute proof, who wanted to see the Father face to face. There were people whom he healed, like the ten lepers, only one of whom returned to give thanks. There were the twelve apostles, one of whom betrayed him, another who denied him, and all of whom forsook him and fled in the hour of his greatest need. He must have suffered greatly when men rejected his message and disappointed his hopes. He wept over Jerusalem, saying, "How often would I—but ye would not."

It has been said that everyone's life is a diary in which a person means to write one story and is forced to write another. So Paul planned to go one way and had to travel another. A young surgeon, fresh from medical school, applied for the post of doctor in a Clydeside village and was rejected. He always said that it was the greatest disappointment of his life, but he added that if he had been appointed, he would probably have spent all his life in a village. Instead he became Sir James Young Simpson, the discoverer of chloroform. Oliver Goldsmith obtained his doctor's degree and found himself penniless. He was glad to make up prescriptions and run errands for charitable druggists. He applied for a minor post at a naval hospital but was rejected. So he began to write, and eight years later he gave to the world *The Vicar of Wakefield,* one of the finest of English novels. It was born of a disappointment.

Nathaniel Hawthorne was discharged from his post in the Customs House at Salem, Massachusetts, and returned home a crushed man. But when he told his wife of his discharge, her only reply was to put pen and ink before him on the desk and say, "Now you can write." Disappointment has often been the spur which has stirred men to high achievement. So it was in the case of the Reverend G. Campbell Morgan. He was turned down for the Wesleyan Methodist ministry and wired to his father one word, "Rejected." Then he wrote in his diary, "Very dark everything seems. Still, He knows best." Quickly came the reply, "Rejected on earth, accepted in heaven. Dad." The

30 • COURAGE TO LIVE

sting of the implied rebuke was more of a spur to courage than a dozen commiserations. It was still a dark horizon, but God was riding the storm, holding in check the better things to come. "I thank God today," Dr. Morgan wrote many years later as he looked back over the years, "for closing that door of hope, because when he turned my feet in another direction, I found the breadth of His commandments and the glory of His service." [1]

God may change our direction, but there is always an open road for us. Paul never reached Spain. He entered Rome but as a prisoner in chains and eventually died there. But does anyone pity him? Pity is the last thing we think of in connection with that tremendous soul. "I will come to you," he said, and he has come in glory beyond his greatest dreams. "I am sure," he wrote to the Roman Christians, "that, when I come unto you, I shall come in the fulness of the blessing of the gospel of Christ" (Romans 15:29). Would he have had that assurance if he had set sail for Spain when he knew that his path pointed to Jerusalem? Suppose he had tried to force God's hand in his life? We dare not think how tragic the result would have been. There are a great many disappointed and embittered people in the world, people who are looking back with nothing but regret and forward with anything but hope. And why? Because they made their way to Spain in opposition to the will of God and in deafness to the call of Jerusalem.

When we are disappointed, we should ask ourselves, "What caused my disappointment?" It may result from the frustration of high ideals, worthy aims, and laudable hopes. We have seen that the greatest characters of the past have suffered from it. On the other hand, disappointment may be due to the frustration of selfish designs and trivial aims. It may be the result of vanity, self-will, jealousy, greed, or selfishness. It may be nothing more than wounded self-feeling.

The dull lead of disappointment can be transmuted into the fine gold of Christian magnanimity. Here is a splendid example. In 1884 a new Chair in Ecclesiastical History was founded in Cambridge. For several years the subject had been taught by Professor H. M. Gwatkin, and not unnaturally he expected to be appointed to the Chair, but instead Mandell Creighton was chosen. The defeated candidate swallowed his disappointment and addressed this noble letter to his successful rival.

Will you allow your rival of yesterday the consolation of giving you to-day

HOW TO FACE DISAPPOINTMENT • 31

an individual and hearty welcome to Cambridge? I envy you the splendid work before you; but it is your work now, not mine.

For twelve years I have taught Ecclesiastical History . . . in Cambridge. I have worked faithfully and to the utmost of my power hitherto, and I trust not without success; and now that my work is taken up by stronger hands than mine, I pray the Lord of all History, before whom we both are standing, to give you health and strength and abundant blessing to carry on far better than myself the . . . work entrusted to your charge.

For myself, I am ready to work under you, and to support you loyally in all that falls to me to do. So far as I know my own heart, no jealousy of yesterday shall ever rise on my side to mar the harmony and friendship in which I ask and hope to live with the first Professor of Ecclesiastical History in Cambridge.[2]

Disappointment may disable us morally and spiritually. It may do for any Christian who has not learned to deal with it what it did for Judas—lead him at last through embitterment of spirit to betray his Lord. The discipline of disappointment in any shape or form is a test of our character. Henry Martyn had given all he had to God—his gift of languages—and God called him to the mission field. Then he fell in love. He was tormented with indecision. His work or his love? How could he ask her to go to India? He chose his work. He bade farewell to Lydia and embarked at Portsmouth. But when the ship unexpectedly stopped at Falmouth, he made an impulsive visit to her home and pleaded with her to come with him. She sent him away with some hope that she might follow him. But when he reached India, he received a letter refusing him. Martyn was stunned by the blow and buried himself in his work. He said, "I wish to have my whole soul swallowed up in the will of God." But soon the dread consumption in his system took him by the throat, and it became a race between his fevered brain and the disease. He died at the age of thirty-one at Tokat in Asia Minor after seven years as a missionary, but his task was completed. The New Testament had been translated into Hindustani, Persian, and Arabic. His life was shadowed by a supreme disappointment, but he made of it a pearl.[3]

To nurse a disappointment only makes it grow, sometimes out of all proportion. It is no use ignoring it. You must tackle it and beat it. We have to resolve, come what may, that we will not allow ourselves to be soured and to go about in the character of a disappointed person. We have to weigh up our disappointments with our blessings. Think of all the things you still have and be thankful. Think of the ways in which others have met their disappointments and try to be like them.

32 • COURAGE TO LIVE

James Hannington, a pioneer Anglican missionary in Africa, was bitterly opposed in his work there, but he wrote, "I refuse to be disappointed. I will only praise."[4] The saints teach us that we must not pronounce too readily on life's disappointments, for, properly accepted, they may lead to the very best we could ever know of God or do for him. How familiar is the experience of longing for Spain and settling for a Roman prison and how less familiar is the transforming of a disappointed dream into an opportunity of serving God's purpose!

The two disciples on the Emmaus Road on the first Easter Day were disappointed men. They were obsessed by the notion of final defeat. Jesus had to shock them out of it. He called them fools. They were dismayed because they were viewing the tragedy of Calvary outside the background of God's eternal purpose. The cross isolated, unrelated to its preface in prophecy and the promise of the ultimate triumph of the crucified, is pure tragedy, but no believer has the right to view it out of its proper context. When Jesus related it to the age-long redemptive purpose of God, their dismay vanished. The cross was no longer a tragedy but a triumph, not a human murder but a divine appointment. So from grieving over it, these men began to glory in it. Without the cross, Christ could never have been the Savior.

The way to meet disappointment is to accept it as Jeremiah did when he said, "This is a grief, and I must bear it" (Jeremiah 10:19). Look your disappointment in the face and ask: How may I transform this liability into an asset? How may I turn this cross into a crown? How may I, confined in a narrow Roman cell and unable to reach the Spain of my dreams, change this prison into a pulpit as Paul did?

There are some verses which I read many years ago which suggest the answer to those questions. They point out that if you take the word "Disappointment" and change the first letter from D to H, it becomes His Appointment. That is not one of the things which argument will prove or preaching confirm. It has to be experienced, to be believed. Our life with God is not an aimless loitering, a fruitless wandering. Our Lord knows the path we must take, and he leads us along the way.

> Disappointment—His appointment
> Change one letter—then I see
> That the thwarting of my purpose
> Is God's better choice for me.

HOW TO FACE DISAPPOINTMENT • 33

His appointment must be blessing,
Though it may come in disguise.
For the end from the beginning
Open to His wisdom lies.

Disappointment—His appointment
No good thing will He withhold.
From denials oft we gather
Treasures of His love untold.

4

How to Triumph over Limitations

"Remember my bonds . . ." Colossians 4:18

This is a subject which includes us all. The study of biography confirms the impression that all human beings are handicapped in one way or another, and the secret of the quality of anyone's spiritual life depends on the way that person deals with his or her limitations. The limitations of life are real and cannot be ignored though they do not always occupy the same place in our thoughts. In youth the sense of limitation is kept very much in the background. Life is so full of possibilities, and it seems to stretch out before us like the open road to the endless fields of high romance. It is only as we get beyond our twenties that we begin to see that, as Job once put it, our way is hedged in so we cannot pass. We cannot hope to know everything and do everything. For one thing, time is against us and the years slip by too quickly to allow us to do more than touch the fringe of all we want to know and do. We realize that our capacity is not as big as we once thought it was. There are very few ten-talent or even five-talent

36 • COURAGE TO LIVE

people; most of us belong to the rank and file with only one talent each.

There are such facts in life as heredity and environment, the circumstances in which we live, our physical and mental makeup, the responsibilities that come upon us in the course of the years so that we find ourselves prevented from doing in life exactly what we like. As we grow older, we see our limitations more clearly. James Payn in an essay on "The Backwater of Life," when deafness and cruel pain were closing all the doors about him, wrote: "It is a strange feeling to one who has been immersed in affairs and as it were in the midstream of what we call life, to find oneself in its backwater, crippled and helpless."[1] As the writer of the book of Lamentations says of God, "He hath hedged me about, that I cannot get out . . ." (Lamentations 3:7).

The apostle Paul had his limitations, not only his imprisonments but also his "thorn in the flesh, the messenger of Satan to buffet me . . ." (2 Corinthians 12:7). No one knows what it was, but we know that Paul, like the rest of us, had to handle a limitation that he prayed to escape but could not evade, that he had to settle down and live with somehow or other. He says to us what he said to the church at Colossae, "remember my bonds." We are all of us in bonds of some kind. There is striking testimony to this truth in Morris L. West's novel, *The Shoes of the Fisherman.* It is the story of Kiril Lakota, once a prisoner of the Communists in Russia and now the pope in Rome. Ruth Lewin asks him: "These stories they print about you, your time in prison, your escape, are they true?" "Yes," he answers, and she goes on: "Now you're in prison again." He nods. "In a way, but I hope to break out of it." Wistfully Ruth continues, "We're all in prison one way or another."[2]

What does the recollection of Paul's bonds suggest about our handling of ours? To begin with, we must make sure that our bonds are real bonds and not elastic bands. They may not be genuine fetters but only elastic bands that can be stretched by a sufficiently resolute wrist. Think how Paul stretched the limitations of his Jewish upbringing and education so that he was able to appeal to the Greek as well as to the Jew and to spread the good news to the uttermost parts of the known world. How skillfully he contrived to overleap barriers which to others would have seemed insuperable! It was his faith that enabled Paul to overcome. That is the task of faith in this world, not to explain things but to overcome. Paul, while in prison,

HOW TO TRIUMPH OVER LIMITATIONS • 37

with no prospect of deliverance, is yet able to talk about God as a Father rich in mercy. He says: "Blessed be the God and Father of our Lord Jesus Christ, who hath blessed us with all spiritual blessings in heavenly places in Christ" (Ephesians 1:3). That is where Paul really lived, not in prison, but in the heavenlies with Christ.

The greatest test of faith comes when life shows its worst side. So often we magnify our limitations instead of regarding them as the pepper and salt of life, to use James Chalmers' phrase. We are apt to imagine that no one else has bonds quite so tight as ours, that no one suffers under such limitations as we do. Dr. John Watson used to tell of a Liverpool merchant who, through no fault of his own, failed in business and came down with a crash from prosperity to poverty. When Dr. Watson called to offer his sympathy, he found his friend in the depths of despair. "Everything has gone," he moaned, "everything!" "That's bad," said Dr. Watson, "so you've lost your reputation?" "No, thank God," said the man, somewhat indignantly, "my name and reputation are unsullied." "Then your wife has left you," suggested Dr. Watson. "My wife has been a perfect brick, loyal and kind and true," replied the man. "Then your children have turned their backs on you?" asked Dr. Watson. "I never seemed to know my children until this happened," said his friend. "They have been so brave and sympathetic. I can't tell you what they mean to me just now." "My dear man," said Dr. Watson, "you told me you had lost everything. Why, you've lost nothing except a bag of gold which doesn't matter. Love, loyalty, comradeship—all the really important things—are yours still. Cheer up and don't be a fool." His bonds were only elastic bands which could be stretched and made easier if only he could have seen them in the right way.

The second thing suggested to us by our recollection of Paul's bonds is that we should accept our bonds as divinely appointed. That is what Paul did. He called himself the prisoner of the Lord. If we want to find true freedom, we must become prisoners of the Lord and we shall find that his service is perfect freedom. Only those who confine themselves within certain limits can really perform the task assigned them. The first rule in art is limitation. Great poetry, great paintings, and great drama are all made by what has been omitted quite as much as by what has been included.

If God hedges up our way and permits some thorn to enter our lives, we may rest assured that his grace is sufficient for all our needs and he can so transfigure the thorn as to make it blossom in our lives

38 • COURAGE TO LIVE

like a rose. How amazingly God has sanctified our hardships and limitations! It is so easy for us to be mastered by our circumstances instead of mastering them. It is tempting to surrender ourselves in a fatalistic sort of way to our limitations instead of rising superior to them. A notable example of a man who rose superior to his handicaps is Robert Louis Stevenson. In a letter to George Meredith he said, "For the last fourteen years I have not had a day's real health. I have wakened sick and gone to bed weary, and I have done my work unflinchingly. The powers have so willed that my battlefield should be this dingy inglorious one of the bed and the physic bottle."[3] Yet how cleverly he concealed the fact of his sufferings in his books, which are full of cheery optimism and Christian courage. Sweet are the uses of adversity if only we face it with courage, gaiety, and the quiet mind.

God is working out his purpose in us and in all his children. Can we not take a long view of things and see our lives in the light of God's purpose and so cheerfully accept our bonds as divinely appointed? Ignatius Loyola was put in prison in Salamanca, and when a friend wrote to him condoling with him on his imprisonment, he replied that it showed him to have little love for Christ in his heart if he thought it so sore a thing to wear bonds for Christ's sake.

Very often, it seems, the most worthwhile things that people do are the results of a visit from God to them in prison. Think of Joseph in Egypt, unjustly cast into prison, and John an exile on the isle of Patmos. John Bunyan wrote *Pilgrim's Progress* in Bedford Jail. Sir Walter Raleigh wrote his *History of the World* when he was imprisoned in the Tower of London. Hemmed in, he was free. He pushed out the walls of his jail until they took in the whole world.

The most important of all the lessons we may learn from our recollection of Paul's bonds is that we should think not so much of what we are bound from as of what we are bound to. Paul's confinement in prison cut him off from travel, but it enabled him to have quiet for meditation and to write some of his most enriching letters. Let us not be too anxious about outward freedom. Dwell on the affirmations of life and not on the negatives. Remember what you can do and not what you cannot do. There are always compensations. As the beautiful Italian proverb has it: "When God shuts a door, he opens a window." One thinks of Beethoven in his deafness writing music for the ears of future ages to enjoy. One recalls John Milton in his blindness writing lines like these:

HOW TO TRIUMPH OVER LIMITATIONS • 39

> . . . Yet I argue not
> Against Heaven's hand or will, nor bate
>   a jot
> Of heart or hope, but still bear up
>   and steer
> Right onward. . . .[4]

Or one turns to another field and thinks of James Watt, the inventor, feeble in body and starving on a few shillings a week, saying, "Of all things in life there is nothing more foolish than inventing."[5] Nearer still in time there is David Livingstone, dragging a fever-stricken body through the wastes of Africa for a dream he had set out to attain. There are prisons in all these illustrations—the stony prison of deafness, the dark prison of blindness, the prisons of sickness and infirmity, but out of these prisons came the furtherance of music, poetry, invention, and discovery, just as out of the prison of Paul came the furtherance of the gospel.

The victories which people have won over their limitations are the greatest in the world. Once when Ole Bull, the great violinist, was giving a concert in Paris, his A string snapped, but he transposed the composition and finished it on three strings. The most thrilling part of the human story on this earth lies in the capacity to handle such a handicap victoriously. Our bonds are guides to divine duties if only we think not so much of what we are bound from as of what we are bound to. Our limitations are also our opportunities. Helen Keller, blind, deaf, and dumb from infancy, once wrote: "I thank God for my handicaps, for through them I have found myself, my work, and my God."[6] In a lighter vein, remember what Emerson's squirrel said to the mountain:

> "If I cannot carry forests on my back,
> Neither can you crack a nut."[7]

That spirit has brought out of small chances some of the most priceless results in human history. Dr. Fosdick has spoken of a friend of his in a midwestern university who told him that in all his years he never heard such cheering as greeted a crippled boy carried in the arms of his companions across the platform on a Commencement Day. Four years before that boy had answered, "Present," at the first roll call of his class. "Stand up," said the professor. "I should like to, sir, but I have not been able to stand up since I was four years old," the boy replied. But by being what he was in a difficult situation, that crippled boy made such an impression on the university that when his

40 • COURAGE TO LIVE

companions carried him up for his diploma, the assembly broke out into cheers such as that college generation had never heard before.[8]

"The foundation of God standeth sure" (2 Timothy 2:19). We always have that to fall back upon. We always have a little more power of resistance than we think. If we hold on long enough, we shall win through, twisted and strained and nearly finished in the end, but we shall win the day. A well-known religious journalist, F. A. Atkins, tells how he lunched one Sunday in a London club with a famous minister who was in sad trouble, unwell and thoroughly tired. "Yet that morning," he writes, "he had preached one of the most searching and inspiring sermons I had ever heard. I laughingly remarked that he always preached best when things were at their worst. He looked at me and said quietly, 'We get help.' I have never forgotten those three words. I have sometimes thought them worth printing as a motto to hang on the wall as a rebuke to our fears and a challenge to our faith. For there is the secret of everything. We get help."[9]

How do we keep going? How have we avoided moral shipwreck? How do we triumph over our limitations? We get help. Christ can give us the courage to keep on and to become the architects and not the victims of circumstance. Have you ever seen a new building in the process of erection covered with scaffolding and then returned a few months later to the same spot and seen the building in all its glory and newness with the scaffolding removed? Circumstances are the scaffolding on which the feet of God's workmen rest while they build and adorn our character. The day will come when God will strike away the scaffolding, the hardships, and the limitations, and in the glory of our new freedom we shall regret nothing that has helped to bring us into the likeness of Jesus Christ. "For our light affliction, which is but for a moment, worketh for us a far more exceeding and eternal weight of glory" (2 Corinthians 4:17). Let us then, remembering the Apostle's bonds, face up to the hard knocks of life and keep the flag bravely flying, reckoning that "the sufferings of this present time are not worthy to be compared with the glory which shall be revealed in us" (Romans 8:18).

5

How to Master Depression

"We are perplexed, but not in despair." 2 Corinthians 4:8

There is no one who has not at some time or other been plagued by depression. We have gray days and low moods when we are a nuisance to ourselves and to everybody about us, days when nothing goes right. There is no beauty in the world, no joy in friendship, and no interest in our work when such a mood is upon us. Depression may spoil our lives and embitter our relationships. Its cause may be physical, a lack of exercise and fresh air. "All work and no play makes Jack a dull boy," as the proverb reminds us. We can drive ourselves too hard. Depression can come from self-pity, like that of the small child, weeping over a broken doll, who said, "I'm sorry for me." We can be obsessed by our own problems and feel that no one has problems as difficult as ours.

Those who rise high often sink low. Strong impulsive natures often fall into fits of depression. We all get discouraged at times and are tempted to say that our work is of no use and abandon it in despair. I

42 • COURAGE TO LIVE

have known days when a weight seems to lie upon my spirit, when all zest has gone out of life, when work has become a weariness and things that once brought joy to me have lost their appeal. But I have learned not to take my depression too seriously. I have recognized that it has some simple cause. It may be the result of physical weariness or mental overstrain. It may be just the reaction of a nature that cannot always be living on the heights. So I have come to know that things are not so bad as they seem to be. The springs of joy have not dried up forever. I have looked in God's direction even though I could not see him, and I have waited until he has brought me again into the light. I have learned to offer even my depression to God, willing to bear it until he removes it, asking only that he may somehow be glorified and that I may be more able because of my experience to help some other child of God. So I have once again been able to stand up to life.

Depression may arise from feelings of guilt. There can be no misery like that of one who feels the pangs of conscience, as Shakespeare shows us in *Macbeth* and Nathaniel Hawthorne in *The Scarlet Letter*. Is there no way of escape? Is there no cure for this sickness of the soul? Is there no deliverance from depression? Of course there is. God never sends a problem without providing a way of escape. In his graphic description of the Slough of Despond in *Pilgrim's Progress,* John Bunyan tells us that it was "such a place as could not be mended," but Help pointed out to Christian that there are certain good and substantial steps through the midst of it, by giving heed to which the good ground might be reached again.

The first of these steps has been found when we realize that these moods of depression are not so singular as we suppose. We tend to imagine that we have been singled out as their special victim. But there are very few of us who never find ourselves in the Slough of Despond. As the spiritual puts it, "Sometimes I'se up, sometimes I'se down, Oh, yes, Lord." Anyone who expects completely to escape low moods is expecting the impossible.

The Bible shows us that even a good person is liable to despair. Elijah, after his triumph over the priests of Baal on Mount Carmel, had to flee for his life from the wrath of Jezebel. We see him alone in the wilderness in a mood of deep depression. He sat down under a juniper tree and prayed God to take away his life. For the moment all the fight had gone out of him. John the Baptist, when he was cast into prison, began to think his whole ministry had been based on some tragic mistake. He sent a message to Jesus asking, "Art thou he that should come or look we for another?"

Many of the psalmists gave themselves up to the unrestrained outpouring of their misery: "O my God, my soul is cast down within me: . . . all thy waves and thy billows are gone over me" (Psalm 42:6-7). "Will the Lord cast off for ever? . . . Is his mercy clean gone for ever? . . . Hath God forgotten to be gracious?" (Psalm 77:7-9). We do not associate perplexity with Paul. Have we not often wished for the same kind of positive faith he possessed? Yet we find him writing to the church at Corinth: "We are perplexed"—it is a very strong word that he uses which means "without a road"—"but not in despair."

John Bunyan gives us not only a picture of the Slough of Despond but also of Doubting Castle and its master, Giant Despair. Christian and Hopeful are oppressed by a sense of failure and by the suggestion of the giant that they should kill themselves or he will do it for them. Bunyan had plenty of chances of meeting Giant Despair in Bedford Jail, and we know from his personal narrative that he did. Think of his characters—Mr. Fearing, Mr. Despondency, Miss Much Afraid, and Mr. Feeble Mind. They were all ready victims of Giant Despair.

Some of us are mastered by our own depressions. The gloomy moods that descend upon us dissolve our inner strength. Deep within us we have not only depressed hours, but we become depressed persons. At the Battle of Shiloh during the Civil War, General Jordan said to General Beauregard: "General, do you not think our troops are very much in the condition of a lump of sugar thoroughly soaked with water, but yet preserving its original shape, though ready to dissolve?"[1] Depressed persons are like that, still retaining their outward shape, but ready to dissolve.

John Wesley's new life began in that glorious experience in the meetinghouse in Aldersgate Street when his heart was strangely warmed and an assurance was given him that Christ had taken away his sins. But within a year of that glowing experience we find him in despair. He even wrote, "I am not a Christian now." Wordsworth in portraying his disappointment in the events of the French Revolution said, "I lost all feeling of conviction, and . . . yielded up moral questions in despair."[2] He had hoped for great things from that stormy time. He had hoped for the birth of brotherhood and freedom. His disappointment disheartened him.

There is nothing wrong in meeting discouragement, but it is fatal to

44 • COURAGE TO LIVE

give way to it. We need not be defeated. God can be an interior source of power greater than ourselves that we can tap. We will have depressed hours, but we need not be depressed persons. All the water in the ocean cannot sink a ship unless it gets inside it. All the despondency in the world cannot swamp our spirits unless we let it in. "Why art thou cast down, O my soul?" asks the psalmist, "and why art thou disquieted in me? hope thou in God . . ." (Psalm 42:5).

The greatest souls in history have had their dark days of depression, but they have not allowed the waves to wash into their souls. Elijah imagined that he was the only person in the world who was upholding God, but he learned that he was not alone: there were seven thousand yet in Israel who had not bowed the knee to Baal, and they were waiting for the lead that Elijah could give. Martin Luther had his day of despair when he felt that the Reformation was a losing cause and that all his work was in vain. But his wife dressed herself in black to surprise him, saying, "Don't you know that God is dead?" It was a salutary lesson for the great reformer. From that day he took heart and would no longer allow despair to eat away his soul.

The second of the steps which lead out of the Slough of Despond was discovered by the psalmist when, after pouring out his misery in a succession of dreary verses, he suddenly shook himself and said, "This is my infirmity." He realized that it was not the world that had gone wrong but only that something had gone wrong with the person who was regarding it so dolefully. A good person is liable to despair but is also forbidden to despair, for to be a depressed person is to be a public liability.

If ever a man might have despaired, it was the apostle Paul. In his second letter to the church at Corinth he gives a record of his sufferings: ". . . in perils of waters, in perils by mine own country-men, in perils by the heathen, in perils in the city, in perils in the wilderness, in perils in the sea, in perils among false brethren; in weariness and painfulness, in watchings often, in hunger and thirst, in fastings often, in cold and nakedness " (2 Corinthians 11:26-27). If any man might have lost heart with good reason, was it not Paul? But he met life with a shout of triumph. "We are troubled on every side, yet not distressed; we are perplexed, but not in despair; persecuted, but not forsaken; cast down, but not destroyed. . . . Therefore seeing we have this ministry . . . we faint not" (2 Corinthians 4:8-9, and 1).

There is only one example of courage that rises higher than that of the Apostle and that is the courage of his Lord and Master. He

HOW TO MASTER DEPRESSION • 45

despaired of no man. Yet what cause for despair he had! What griefs, disappointments, and seeming failures were his lot! But on the eve of Gethsemane and in the shadow of the cross he is talking about his joy, the joy that no person could take away from him.

Percy Ainsworth in one of his sermons says: "Of all the luxuries of life, perhaps the most unwarrantable and in the end the most wasteful and costly is the luxury of despair. And how many there are who indulge in it! A man may have to walk in a deep shadow, but he has no right to sit in it."[3] There is nothing so fatal as to lose heart. Once you believe that you are going to be defeated, you need not trouble to fight. The battle is lost before you begin. Get into your mind that nothing will come of your efforts and you will make none. Failure without is bad enough, but it is failure within that ruins a person.

> "Man, what is this and why art thou despairing?
> God shall forgive thee all but thy despair."[4]

Why is despair excluded from the list of pardonable offenses? It is because we are saved by hope, and despair is the death of hope. Saint Teresa, who knew the gray days of the soul, tells us how sometimes her darkness would be in a moment dispersed. "When the sun rose, I saw how silly I had been."[5] It is a sound rule never to accept the verdict of our melancholy and depressed hours. Depression destroys our power of seeing things in the right perspective. Elijah under the juniper tree and John the Baptist in prison were in no condition to estimate the value of their influence or the success or failure of their cause. No angel knew his business better than the angel who told Elijah to eat and drink and go to sleep and ask himself how much he was worth another day.

Action is one of the best methods of shaking off idle shadows from the soul. The worst thing in which we can indulge is an orgy of self-pity, and the best thing we can do is to do whatever duty lies before us. John Keble gave sound advice when he said, "When you find yourself overpowered by melancholy, the best way is to go out and do something kind to somebody or other."[6] When we see what others have to suffer, we become ashamed to mention our small troubles. Depression cannot live under the same roof with honest activity. When John Bright sat in gloom and grief mourning the death of his young wife, Richard Cobden went to visit him. It was during the first terrible days of the Industrial Revolution. After expressing his sympathy with his friend in his loss, Cobden said, "There are

46 • COURAGE TO LIVE

thousands of homes in England at this moment where wives, mothers and children are dying of hunger. When the first paroxysm of your grief is past I would advise you to come with me, and we will never rest until the Corn Law is repealed."[7] The mood of depression was mastered by the response to the call of duty.

This is the third of those good and substantial steps that lead out of the Slough of Despond. "Blessed is he that considereth the poor: the Lord will deliver him in time of trouble" (Psalm 41:1). I take the psalmist to mean that there is no surer way of getting relief from a troubled heart and a gloomy mind than to get busy in some unselfish service. There are always people who are much worse off than we are and who stand in need of our help and comfort. Did not Job find that his captivity was turned when he prayed for his friends?

"Why has this trouble come upon me?" you may ask. That is God's business and he knows his business. "How am I to meet this trouble?" That is your business. Paul discovered the secret of invincible living. "BUT NOT"—that was the secret of victory. "I am harried on every side, but not hemmed in." There is always a gap through the surrounding hosts of evil through which Christ can come. There is always one line of communication that is never cut, the line that leads to Christ. He can turn defeat into victory and make us super-conquerors. You will be buffeted as you go through life, but you need never be knocked out. Some men are like drums: you never hear of them until they are beaten.

Take, for example, Sir Walter Scott. Having built Abbotsford, he was about to retire in middle life and live in ease and comfort. Then the blow fell and he found himself involved in bankruptcy to the tune of one hundred thousand pounds. Let his diary tell the courage of this brave soul. "I feel neither dishonored nor broken down by the news I have received. Discouragement is to me a tonic and a bracer."[8] He set himself to pay off every penny of the debt with his own right hand. From his pen there came one after another of the Waverley novels, and the world of literature has been forever enriched because of the noble way in which Sir Walter transformed his failure into victory.

If sometimes you think that you have been harshly dealt with, if sometimes you think that God has not given you a square deal, if sometimes you are inclined to bemoan your lot in life, take a long look at Calvary and then go back and shoulder your cross like a man. Transform that symbol of defeat into victory. Dr. Fosdick tells of a

HOW TO MASTER DEPRESSION • 47

friend of his who was stricken with infantile paralysis in her youth. Someone sympathizing with her said, "Affliction does so color the life." "Yes," she replied gallantly, "and I propose to choose the color."[9] There was a Christian rising above despair, refusing to give way to self-pity. If we only ask him, God will give us the garment of praise for the spirit of heaviness. "Why art thou cast down, O my soul? and why art thou disquieted in me? hope thou in God: for I shall yet praise him for the help of his countenance" (Psalm 42:11).

6

Fear—Friend or Foe?

"Why are you afraid? Have you no faith?"
Mark 4:40, RSV

How can I not be afraid? I live in a world where no one knows what tomorrow may bring, a world "where men's hearts are failing them for fear and for expectation of the things that are coming" (Luke 21:26, paraphrase). Suppose I should lose my health, or suppose those outward comforts and conveniences on which life seems to depend for its well-being were to be withdrawn? Suppose I should be called upon to bear some burden of pain or find myself suddenly face to face with death? I am almost afraid to be happy today for fear that my happiness should not last till tomorrow. My joy in the comradeship that has been given me is darkened by my fear of the loneliness that may come. All manner of formless fears haunt my soul—fears of some dark thing that may swoop upon me from the unknown, some sad news that I may hear at any time. How can I not be afraid when this shadow of insecurity rests over my life?

Fear attacks one person in one way and another in a different way.

50 • COURAGE TO LIVE

Look at the people you meet in the course of a few hours. Many of them are living or working in fear. The mother is afraid for her children. The father is afraid for his business. The clerk is afraid of losing his job. There is hardly a man who is not afraid that some other man will do him a bad turn. There is hardly a woman who is not afraid that things she desires may be denied her or that what she loves may be snatched away. There is not a home nor an office nor a factory nor a school nor a church in which some fear is not threatening the happiness of the people who go in and out.

Centuries ago a keen observer of human behavior who knew that fear in one form or another is the scourge of the human race wrote: "Say to them that are of a fearful heart, Be strong, fear not" (Isaiah 35:4). One greater than Isaiah saw that fears were destroying the serenity of men and women, and He said to them, "Fear not, little flock; for it is your Father's good pleasure to give you the kingdom" (Luke 12:32). Once Jesus, tired out after a long day of preaching, suggested to the disciples that they should secure a boat and cross over to the other side of the Sea of Galilee. As they set sail, Jesus laid his head on the helmsman's pillow in the stern of the boat and, rocked by the gentle motion of the waves, fell fast asleep. When they were in the middle of the lake, a terrific storm burst upon them. Panic seized the disciples and they roused Jesus, crying, "Master, carest thou not that we perish?" Quietly Jesus turned to the storm and stilled it. He did this not because he was afraid of the storm but because of its effect on his disciples. Then he rebuked them, saying, "Why are ye so fearful? how is it that ye have no faith?" (see Mark 4:35-40).

In these words Jesus was expressing his disappointment in the disciples because they had allowed themselves to be stampeded by fear. Jesus meant that, if they had been possessed by true faith in God, they would not have been afraid of physical death. They would have been sustained by the assurance that even though their bodies had found a resting place on the bottom of the lake, their souls would have been safe in God's keeping. It is quite likely that the peril in which they found themselves was due just as much to the fact that they had become paralyzed by fear as it was to the storm that raged about them.

Fear is universal. There is no such thing as a person who does not know what fear is. There is enough happening in the world, let alone in our private lives, to cause us to fear. The important thing is to learn how to master it. Psychologists have warned us against our misuse of

FEAR—FRIEND OR FOE? • 51

the word "fear." They tell us that it is not an instinct but an instinctive emotion. They say that if only we understood the service which fear renders, we would not speak of it as if it were a foe but as a friend.

Fear can be a friend. It is not in itself an evil thing. It may be helpful and constructive. It can give mobility to the body and alertness to the mind. It is a lifesaver. Were it not for fear, thousands of lives would be lost through carelessness. Who would be willing to trust oneself to the pilot of an airplane who knew nothing of fear? Fear is the elemental alarm system of the human organism. We make provision for a rainy day because we are afraid of what might happen in the future. We look both ways before crossing the road because we are afraid of a traffic accident. One of the things which every mother worries about concerning her children is that they have no fear. They never see danger. They have to be taught that there are some things in life of which they do well to be afraid.

Fear of ignorance makes for knowledge. Fear of disease inspires medical research. Fear of tyranny prompts the struggle for liberty. Fear of war and its ravages led to the formation of the United Nations. Fear of the consequences keeps countless men and women from wrongdoing. Fear has been a faithful servant of humankind through all the long development of our race.

No thinking or responsible person should live without wholesome fears. Fear gives us warning of the approach of danger, so that we may be on our guard. Someone has said that, rightly understood, fear is the father of courage and the mother of safety. Life is a difficult and dangerous business. Accidents do happen. Trouble is something we cannot avoid. Fortunes can be lost and so can health. Bereavement will overtake us all some day. There is no point in telling people that there is nothing to be afraid of: it is not true. Dr. Robert J. McCracken tells of a mother who wanted her boy to run an errand for her: "It meant crossing a field in which there was a belligerent goat. The boy was afraid even to enter the field and his mother [who was a Christian Scientist] kept saying to him, . . . 'Why should you be afraid? You know that nothing can hurt you. You know that there is no such thing as evil or pain.' 'Yes,' he answered, 'I know. But how do I know that the goat knows?' There was sound common sense in his reply. . . . Evil and pain are realities. The things that cause fear are never very far from any one of us. It is fear itself that must be met and mastered. Was Franklin Roosevelt speaking out of his personal experience, his own experience of physical pain and afflictions when

52 • COURAGE TO LIVE

he made the remark . . . 'The only thing we have to fear is fear itself.'?" [1]

Fear may be a friend, but it can also be a foe. Fear, as the Bible says, has torment. We have to make a distinction between natural fear and neurotic fear. The fear that is natural is a friend, for it puts us on the alert. The fear that is neurotic is a foe, for it paralyzes us. In these days, neurotic fear has grown to such proportions that it overshadows the life of multitudes and robs them of physical and mental health. When fear overshoots the mark, it becomes a destructive force. It impairs human judgments, reduces efficiency, and robs persons of hope. Fear turns into phobia. A phobia is a fear attached to objects not in themselves dangerous. So we have claustrophobia, the fear of closed places; agoraphobia, the fear of open places; acrophobia, the fear of heights. In fact, there are more than seventy phobias listed in the dictionary, all of them abnormal, irrational fears.

My pastoral experience convinces me that man's chief enemy is not sin or sorrow, for sin can be forgiven and sorrow healed, but fear. It was the first enemy that attacked man. When at the beginning Adam and Eve broke the commandment of God and then heard the voice of God walking in the garden, they were afraid and hid themselves among the trees of the garden. Paul tells us that death is the last enemy. Since we fear death, fear is therefore our first and last enemy. Fear is indispensable as a healthy vigilance, but it must be held in and kept in its place if it is not to degenerate into a morbid panic. Fear strikes at the heart of a happy life. It produces intense mental suffering. It undermines our strength, poisons our hope, destroys our courage, and unfits us for the duties of our daily lives.

Fear of what may happen is often more destructive of happiness than the actual evil thing that does happen. An Oriental proverb says: "The plague killed five thousand but fear of the plague killed fifty thousand." A lady was on the verge of a nervous collapse. She insisted that someone kept following her. No, she did not see him, but she heard footsteps every time she went for a walk. A doctor at the Peterborough Hospital solved the mystery. She was wearing her hearing aid backwards. What she had thought were footsteps were the sounds of her own heartbeats. When we do not listen to our faith, we turn in upon ourselves and mistake our fears for realities.

When fear really takes grip of a human mind, it can distort the loveliest things and turn even the truth against itself. Dr. W. E.

FEAR—FRIEND OR FOE? • 53

Sangster gives an example of this. He tells of a doctor who was talking to a new patient one day. "In great alarm the patient mentioned a rare and deadly disease of the liver and claimed to be suffering from it. 'Nonsense!' protested the doctor. 'You are not suffering from that. In fact, you wouldn't know whether you had it or not. It is a disease which gives no discomfort at all.'

'That's just it!' gasped the poor patient. 'My last doctor told me that. That is how I know I have it. I feel quite well!'"[2]

When fear inhibits us, we can never live at our best. How then shall we master our fears? Whenever there is a persistent fear in your life, carry it out into the daylight and examine it critically. Never try to put it out of your mind, but place it in the very center. Examine it with your God-given intelligence, and you will rob it of its power to enslave and torture you.

There is no shame in being afraid. The shame lies in surrendering to our fears. First ask, "What am I afraid of?" and then, "Why am I afraid?" Look your fears in the face. Fear faced is fear lost, and fear lost is security gained. The story of the little boy who used to suffer nightmares because of his fear of a big tiger that came toward him in his sleep is worth repeating. A wise psychiatrist took him in his arms and talked to him about his imaginary visitor. He told him that it was really a friendly tiger and that the next time he came, he should reach out and touch him and say, "Hello, old chap." That night the doctor and the parents watched the boy after he had fallen asleep. They saw his little body grow tense for a moment and then a hand go out as if it were patting something. Then the boy said, "Hello, old chap," and he turned over and fell into a deep, refreshing sleep.[3] Never fly from a fear but face it, and the tiger will become a lamb and the foe become a friend.

The causes of fear lie largely within ourselves. We are afraid of ourselves more than we are of our enemies. Paul was afraid of himself. He wrote to the Corinthians that he was afraid that, after having preached to others, he himself might be a castaway. Job cried out in his agony, "The thing which I greatly feared is come upon me . . . " (Job 3:25). We are afraid of failure. We want health, happiness, wealth, success; and if there is one thing we are afraid of more than any other, it is that they may not come to us or that, having come, they may be taken from us. The real root of our fear is that we are too wrapped up in ourselves. Only when we fix our hearts on things that really matter shall we be free from fear. One thing that

54 • COURAGE TO LIVE

may save us from being oppressed by our fears is to talk them over with some Christian friend or a minister or doctor.

Do you remember Mr. Fearing in *Pilgrim's Progress* who was always afraid that "he should come short of whither he had a desire to go." He could not pluck up courage to cross the Slough of Despond; yet he would not go back. When at last he did get over, he could hardly believe it. He was afraid to knock at the wicket gate or to make himself known at the Interpreter's House, though he had no trouble with the Hill of Difficulty or the Valley of Humiliation. In the Valley of the Shadow he was nearly ready to die of fear, crying out that the hobgoblins would have him. And when at last he came to the edge of the river where there was no bridge, there comes the stroke of genius in the story, for Bunyan says: "The water of the river was lower at this time than ever before, so Mr. Fearing went over at last, not much above wetshod." We would like to be Mr. Greatheart or Mr. Standfast or Mr. Valiant for the Truth. Yet so many of us only succeed in being Mr. Fearing. Our anxieties are concerned with the things we are afraid are going to happen. Our fears are fears of "coming short of whither we have a desire to go." Yet how gently Mr. Fearing is dealt with in Bunyan's allegory. Things are made easy for him.

The Christian religion teaches us to look at fear in the light of our Lord's presence. Faith conquers fears about ourselves, our loved ones, and the unknown future. The antidote to fear is faith. The secret of fearlessness is confidence in God. Are you afraid of life? As a minister I have spent a good deal of time in hospitals dealing with people who are very ill but not ill enough to die. Some of them are more frightened to live than to die. The cure for fear that I have always offered them is, "Take it to God." I would quote the words of the psalmist: "I sought the Lord, and he heard me, and delivered me from all my fears" (Psalm 34:4). One of life's greatest lessons is that God is greater than our fears just as he is mightier than our sins. His world is a place where nothing evil can happen to us except by our own consent. Faith and fear cannot live together in one heart and life. At the time of the Dunkirk disaster in 1941 when Britain was afraid of a German invasion, someone wrote this inscription over the entrance to the Hind's Head Hotel in Dover. "Fear knocked. Faith answered, No one is here."[4] As Isaiah puts it: "I will trust and not be afraid; for the Lord Jehovah is my strength and my song; he also is become my salvation" (Isaiah 12:2). Fear is self-centered. Faith is God-centered.

FEAR—FRIEND OR FOE? • 55

Fear turns us toward ourselves. Faith turns us toward God. "What time I am afraid," says the psalmist, "I will trust in thee," and then he continues, ". . . in God I have put my trust; I will not fear what flesh can do unto me" (Psalm 56:3-4).

It is only by the exercise of faith that we shall ever master our fears, that is, by the quiet confidence that whatever comes we cannot drift beyond God's love and care, that he will be there to see us through, that the strain will bring the strength. Look into the mirror of the perfect life of Jesus, and you will see that there is fulfilled in him the promise of Scripture that "perfect love casteth out fear." Our Lord lived free from every foolish fear. He had such complete trust in his Father's love and power that he could live without the disablement of fear. One of his favorite phrases was "Fear not." "Fear not, ye are of more value than many sparrows." "Fear not them that can kill the body." "Fear not; only believe." "Fear not, I am the first and the last and the living one." He plainly told his friends that in the world they would have tribulation, but he also said to them, "Let not your heart be troubled, neither let it be afraid."

Jesus was free from fear because he was confident that his Father was on the throne and that all his Father's purposes were loving, wise, and good. He was free from fear also because he believed that his Father would turn all the disasters of life into spiritual success, even to turning his cross of shame into a throne of glory. So when the fear of anything comes upon you, place yourself in the hands of God, and over the chasm of the years you will hear the voice of the Master saying, "Be not afraid. I am with thee."

> When 'tis deeply rooted here
> Perfect love shall cast out fear,
> Fear doth servile spirits bind;
> Jesu's is a *noble* mind.[5]

Go bravely into the unknown future with Jesus. When you walk with him, fears fall before you. He bends over the unrest of your fearful heart and speaks that word which he spoke long ago to the disciples whose hearts were more troubled than the waters of the Galilean lake, "Peace, be still."

7

A Home for the Lonely

"God setteth the solitary in families . . ."
Psalm 68:6, KJV
"The God who brings the lonely home . . ."
Psalm 68:6, Moffatt

Some time ago a "Peanuts" cartoon revealed Linus admitting that he is afraid to go into the public library. His friend, Charlie Brown, tries to comfort him by explaining that everybody is lonely in some place or another. Linus counters this with the question, "What's your place?" To which Charlie replies, "Earth." Everyone has experienced this deep existential loneliness. There is a sense in which everyone is lonely. A person's struggles with self, with temptations, doubts, and fears are fought out in the lonely fastnesses of the soul. Each has a different road to travel, different trials, and different joys, and these differences are invisible barriers between us so that even in fellowship we walk apart. "The heart knoweth his own bitterness; and a stranger doth not intermeddle with his joy" (Proverbs 14:10).

Loneliness is one of the major social evils of our day. It is on the increase in that twice as many people are living alone today compared with twenty-five years ago. I think of elderly, often unmarried,

58 • COURAGE TO LIVE

women who live in apartments hardly ever visited by anyone. Day after day one of them who kept a diary wrote on page after page, "No one called." I think of the loneliness of an only child, the loneliness of a young man who goes to the university, who was so bright when he had only the other boys of his school to compete with, but who now finds himself very ordinary and solitary because the standard of ability has jumped to university level. I think of the loneliness of a young person in the first weeks in a bank or an office or a factory. It is easy to get into bad company if it promises an end to loneliness. You would think that marriage would end loneliness, but many a young wife is suddenly cut off from the associates in her business or profession and has many lonely hours. I have seen a young bride full of Christian ideals gradually lose them because it is too lonely to maintain them. Her husband has no use for them. The circle in which they move despises religion. So she gives up going to church and saying her prayers.

Loneliness is no respecter of age. There is the loneliness of youth. Youth is a time of stress and strain, fear and uncertainty. It is a search for one's selfhood which means breaking away from dependence on one's parents. One who walks this road feels lonely and misunderstood, at times almost driven to despair of life itself. There is the loneliness of middle age, when one comes to grips with frustrated dreams and lost ideals. There is the loneliness of old age. Too many people feel that life has pushed them aside. They miss their work, their children, and many of the activities they once enjoyed. They feel unwanted and unloved. Their ideas are often regarded as old-fashioned. Their advice is never sought. Many old people wish they could die, and secretly this wish is sometimes shared by those who look after them.

We must not confuse loneliness with solitariness. Loneliness expresses the pain of being alone: solitude expresses the glory of being alone. You can tramp alone over the hills or sit quietly by the sea. That is not loneliness. Nature can speak to your soul. "I wandered lonely as a cloud," said Wordsworth and in his solitary excursions he saw deep into the heart of things. You can sit alone in your room surrounded by books and enjoy the fellowship of those silent friends. A healthy soul is not afraid of solitude. It demands it. It knows the truth that lies in the saying, "Religion is what a man does with his solitariness." In the solitary place of the human heart is to be found the meeting place of God and the individual. Each of us, like

A HOME FOR THE LONELY • 59

our Lord, needs to go apart from others from time to time to recollect ourselves and to talk with God.

We are hermit spirits and it is necessary that we should be. Solitude reminds us of our dignity, of our individual worth as a soul. There are too many who never take time to be alone, who never follow the advice of the psalmist: "Stand in awe, and sin not: commune within your own heart upon your bed, and be still" (Psalm 4:4). If we are to grow by reason of our experience, we must be sufficiently alone in it to feel deeply the impact of life and to learn its meaning.

But the soul that feels itself alone should not also be lonely. "God setteth the solitary in families." He provides natural associations which, in part, meet our need. Even Jesus felt acutely the need of companionship. He chose the twelve that they might be with him. That is why he was so sad when he found Peter, James, and John asleep in the garden. "Could ye not watch with me one hour?" (Matthew 26:40). That is the cry of a soul that is strong enough to be alone, but is disappointed that it should also be condemned to loneliness.

We cannot intrude upon the intimacies of another's experience, but that does not mean that we are powerless to help. A mother is not useless to her child because she cannot bear its pain. If a man is to win through temptation and reach nobility of character, he can succeed only if he is surrounded by the right kind of friends. The task of the church is to be a home for the lonely, surrounding people with loving friendships. We must not allow our shyness or reserve to keep us from rendering this service to our fellow-worshipers. The fellowship of the church is a great defense against the perils and temptations of loneliness.

There are many ways in which people can be lonely. Sometimes it is due to the physical absence of loved ones. When the poet Rupert Brooke sailed from Liverpool to America in 1913, there was nobody to see him off. So he gave sixpence to a little boy playing around the docks and asked him to wave his handkerchief to him until the vessel was out in midstream. The ache of loneliness was in that bargain. When everybody else had friends to wish them Godspeed, the one man who was alone could not escape his loneliness. He clutched at the mercenary friendship of a ragged boy who kept the contract by straining his eyes over the widening water and waving until his newfound friend was out of sight. The last comment made by the lonely man on the ship was, "I had my sixpennyworth."[1] Our

60 • COURAGE TO LIVE

loneliness is most widespread when those who have helped us to forget that we are alone have left us, either by separation or death. Death makes an emptiness against the sky.

There is the loneliness of the height when one is called to the leadership of others, to the quest of a new truth, or to the vision of a new ideal. When the Prince Consort died, Tennyson wrote of the lonely splendor in which his death left the crown. Queen Victoria herself has told how, on one of her last interviews with the aged poet, he said to her, "You are so alone on that height: it is terrible."[2] The king, the statesman, and the scientist all know the loneliness which, for the moment, one must bear without support. The prophet Jeremiah knew it, for he wrote, "I sat alone because of thy hand . . ." (Jeremiah 15:17).

There is the loneliness in which great decisions are made. The choices that fashion character, that determine one's conduct and shape one's destiny; the choice of a career, of one's life partner, and of one's faith are made alone. Others may suggest or advise, but the final decision rests with the individual. Alan Moorehead, in his book *Eclipse,* describes the consultations between the service chiefs on the eve of D Day in World War II. On the early morning of June 4, in view of the unpromising weather report, the first move was postponed for twenty-four hours. In the evening the leaders met again, reports were received and opinions given, but it was impossible to reach a clear decision. "Suddenly Eisenhower came forward,'This is a decision which I must make alone,' he said. 'After all that is what I am here for.' The meeting waited. Then the commander-in-chief said, 'We will sail tomorrow.'"[3] We have to take similar, if less drastic, responsibility for the decisions we make.

A Christian must often stand alone, a solitary witness to the truth. There is an old hymn which says:

> Dare to be a Daniel,
> Dare to stand alone,
> Dare to have a purpose firm,
> And dare to make it known.

We may have to confront a hostile or an indifferent environment in our homes or our places of business. We have to cherish and proclaim ideals of life and conduct that are challenging and perhaps distasteful to others. This loneliness is bound up with our vocation, the loneliness of the height.

There is also the loneliness of the deep, the loneliness of despair or

A HOME FOR THE LONELY • 61

depression following a season of failure, the loneliness of temptation or of guilt, the loneliness of death. You can feel lonely in a crowd. It is not a crowd that creates the sense of companionship but sympathy, the fellowship of kindred minds. The multitude may throng about us and yet every fiber of our being may ache for the touch which says, "I know, I understand." That was why the woman in the Gospels, in the midst of the crowd that surged around Jesus, said, "If I may but touch his garment, I shall be whole" (Matthew 9:21).

Sin brings loneliness to the soul. It separates us from our closest friends. It separates us from our best selves. It separates us from peace of mind. Most of all, it separates us from God. Judas Iscariot, who betrayed his Lord, knew that kind of loneliness. John tells us that at the Last Supper in the upper room after Judas had received the sop, he went out immediately; "and it was night" (John 13:30). It was night in more senses than one, for there is a night of the soul that is more dreadful than the darkest hour before the dawn. This is the night which the Ancient Mariner in Samuel Coleridge's poem speaks of when he says:

> O Wedding-Guest! This soul hath been
> Alone on a wide wide sea:
> So lonely 'twas, that God himself
> Scarce seeméd there to be.

It is in a world like this with so many kinds of loneliness that the Master has promised to be with his disciples: "Lo, I am with you always." He is the great Companion. God draws us back to himself again and again, for he is the homeland of the soul. He has promised, "I will never leave thee, nor forsake thee" (Hebrews 13:5). No one is naturally a solitary unit: each person belongs to a family. What is it that makes us lonely? Is it not our longing? We may be by ourselves without being lonely, but as soon as we are conscious of loneliness, it is because we are conscious of longing. We long for the fellowship which is our right. "And the Lord God said, It is not good that man should be alone . . . ." (Genesis 2:18). Separation from God makes us conscious of utter loneliness in the hour of deep spiritual crisis. God brings the lonely home when they turn their faces homeward.

The psalmist cries, "Turn thou to me, and be gracious to me; for I am lonely and afflicted" (Psalm 25:16, RSV). Dr. Moffatt translates this cry into modern speech, "Turn to me and have pity, for I am lonely and low; relieve the anguish of my heart, free me from all this pressure." May it not be that God makes us lonely in order that we

62 • COURAGE TO LIVE

may turn to him? We can never be lonely in God's fellowship. "For me to live is Christ" (Philippians 1:21), said Paul, and the friendship of Christ was so intense for him that even in prison he had society. One of his phrases is, "The Lord stood with me." He was in Rome, defenseless and alone. His Christian friends had left him. He was surrounded by enemies and under sentence of death. But he wrote to Timothy: "All . . . forsook me. . . . Notwithstanding the Lord stood with me, and strengthened me" (2 Timothy 4:16-17). It is the assurance of the nearness of that Presence that destroys all feeling of loneliness.

Christ can help us in our loneliness, for he knew loneliness as no one ever knew it before or has known it since. His loneliness was something essential to his greatness, something that he endured for us that we might never be utterly alone. How many among the multitudes cared anything for the things that were nearest to his heart? "Ye seek me . . . because ye did eat of the loaves, and were filled" (John 6:26). So little did they understand him, that they would have taken him away by force and made him king. When he told them it was not for this that he had come, "many of his disciples went back, and walked no more with him" (John 6:66). Jesus must have longed for the support of the religious leaders of his day, but his message of love only stung them into a deep hatred and they plotted his death. When he turned to the twelve, whom he had chosen for companion- ship, there was little ease for the ache of his heart. "I have yet many things to say unto you, but ye cannot bear them now" (John 16:12). In the garden at the time of his greatest need, they all forsook him and fled. Not even when Jesus turned where in their loneliness men have often turned for comfort—to home and friends—was there any healing for his hurt. His brethren did not believe on him. This would deepen his sense of loneliness. Was he not speaking out of the fullness of his pained heart when he said, "A man's foes shall be they of his own household" (Matthew 10:36)?

In the upper room Jesus said to his friends: "Ye . . . shall leave me alone: and yet I am not alone, because the Father is with me" (John 16:32). Though all others had left him; yet in that solitary communion with the Father, Jesus found strength for his hard way. "He that sent me is with me," he said, "the Father hath not left me alone" (John 8:29). There is a revealing word in John's Gospel where he tells what happened after the Feast of Tabernacles. "Every man went unto his own house. Jesus went unto the mount of Olives" (John 7:53–8:1).

A HOME FOR THE LONELY • 63

When no earthly door had its welcome for him, he went to the mount to talk face to face with God. From the clamor of tongues and the rush of distractions he made his escape to the best company of all. It brought him peace and victory. His face shone because he had seen the Father's face. His voice spoke with grace and power because he had listened to the Father's voice.

When the lonely experiences of life come to us, when we face our trial hour, when we crave for sympathy as others crave for water in a dry and thirsty land where no water is, when we tread our Gethsemane, we remember the lonely Christ and are comforted. Robertson of Brighton, the famous Anglican preacher of the last century, was a lonely man. He was bitterly persecuted for views that are now widely held. As his brief life sped away, his friends became fewer, but the great Companion, the Friend that sticketh closer than a brother, came nearer than ever. "I am alone," he wrote in a letter, "and shall be till I die, and I am not afraid to be alone in the majesty of darkness which His Presence peoples with a crowd. A sublime feeling of a Presence comes about me at times which makes inward solitariness a trifle to talk about."[4]

Christ leads us through no darker rooms than he went through before. This is the gospel of the lonely Christ for all lonely souls. It is the assurance that we are understood, that when we are most alone, there is a Companion at our side, that we, too, in life's darkest valley need fear no evil, for the God who brings the lonely home is with us.

8

Time—Tyrant or Servant?

"Redeeming the time . . ." Ephesians 5:16

If you were asked, "What is the time?", you would consult your watch and answer quickly. But if you were asked, "What is time?", how would you answer? There is a mystery about time which has fascinated the world's best thinkers. Time is elastic. Some days stretch out endlessly while others go by in a flash. The length of a day has no fixed value. It depends upon what you are doing. A day may seem long because you are waiting for some anticipated pleasure or because you are dreading something unpleasant. An hour spent in a hospital corridor waiting the result of an operation may seem an eternity, but to a pair of lovers an hour is gone before they know it. People talk about "killing time." They indulge in what they call "pastimes" and they behave as though time were a commodity of which they could never run short. To live right is to live in such a way that yesterday, today, and tomorrow add up to something useful and creative.

66 • COURAGE TO LIVE

There is given to each of us born into this world the priceless treasure of time. We each have the same ration of days, hours, and minutes. Have you ever paused to consider how time is spent? Suppose we sleep eight hours a night—that means we spend a third of our lives asleep. If we spend only an hour at meals, it means that in any one year we spend the equivalent of fifteen days doing nothing but eat. It is one of life's most daunting experiences simply to reckon up the time we spend on things.

Time is God's most sacred gift and our most valuable possession. We get only so much time. To everyone there is an allotment of time in which one may reach full maturity as a person and render such service as is possible to others and leave a mark upon the world. Nothing can buy us any more time. It must therefore be husbanded and used with care. The years and the days and the hours have a way of coming and going so quickly that we seem to lose track of them. A teacher in a New York school received a note from a harried mother: "Please excuse Johnny being late to school today. Nine o'clock came sooner than we expected." It is not only that nine o'clock comes sooner than we expected, but tomorrow comes, maturity comes, middle age comes, and old age comes sooner than we expected. We find ourselves wondering what has happened to the days and the years and where we have misplaced them.

God gives us all the same twenty-four hours each day. The difference between people is largely the use they make of the same hours and minutes. Someone has said that our best confessions of faith are not our creeds but our date books. Here are listed the things to which we give time and therefore our lives. The average person never uses more than 20 percent of one's capacity, and in a large measure that is because a person handles time without a sense of stewardship. Peter Drucker, the well-known American management consultant, has an article, "How to Manage Your Time," in which he calls it "everybody's No. 1 problem." Most businessmen, he says, actually control less than 25 percent of their working hours, because they allow themselves to be interrupted too casually, because they are such poor delegators, and because they do not plan sufficiently. Time for them is a tyrant instead of a servant.

We must learn to be time-conscious, not in the conventional sense of the term, keeping an eye on the clock, but in the Christian sense, that is, to be aware of the shortness and the uncertainty of our lives but also to appreciate God's gift of today and, as Kipling put it, to

"fill the unforgiving minute
With sixty seconds' worth of distance run." [1]

The use of our time, like the use of our talents and our money, is a true index of our soul. We cannot redeem the past, the years wasted in trivial living and self-indulgence. We cannot and we need not, for God has redeemed them for us by the sacrifice of Christ. We cannot redeem the future. No amount of praying or giving can reserve a place in heaven for us. God cannot be bribed. But we can redeem the present by letting God redeem us. Today we can take him at his word, accept from him the gift of his only Son, and in return we will no longer need to worry about time or the passage of time because, whatever our calling, all our time will henceforth be devoted to Christ.

We do not know how much time God has allotted to us, but this we know—that he can help us to redeem our time today and that in this new life with Christ in which we shall belong wholly to him, he will give us, in every sense of the word, the time of our lives. We can sing in the words of Charles Wesley's birthday hymn, celebrating his conversion:

> My remnant of days
> I spend in His praise
> Who died the whole world to redeem.
> Be they many or few,
> My days are His due,
> And they all are devoted to Him. [2]

A large proportion of our time will be spent in our daily work. As Christians our working time belongs to God. Whatever our work may be, God wants our best and will make use of it. Work done grudgingly is servitude; work done willingly is service; work done lovingly is a sacrament. Much of the work that we have to do is sheer mechanical drudgery. The temptation is to get through it somehow with our eyes on the leisure that awaits us. But Christians think of their jobs as their first contribution to the kingdom of heaven and make of their daily work an offering to God. Dr. Leslie Weatherhead tells of a girl who worked in a chocolate factory and who had been converted. She was asked what difference her conversion made to her job. She had been working under a forewoman with whom she found it very difficult to get along. "It's quite different now," she said, "I make chocolates for God." [3] In an English country churchyard is to be found this inscription on a tombstone: "Here lies the body of Andrew Murray who cobbled shoes to the glory of God in this village for forty

68 • COURAGE TO LIVE

years." He put in good leather, did the job well, and so helped God to answer the prayers of His people for health in wet weather.

Some people tithe their money. Why should we not with equal reason tithe our time? I have read of a Dr. Nowel, sometime dean of St. Paul's Cathedral in London, who not only gave away a tenth of his income in charity but also devoted a tenth of his time to recreation. Here is his epitaph: "He died February 13, 1601, being aged 95 years, 44 of which he had been Dean of St. Paul's Cathedral. His age had neither impaired his hearing nor weakened his memory nor made any of the faculties of his mind weak or useless."

We cannot work all the time. God has given every one of us the capacity to laugh, to play, to share life's lighter moments with another. In such play and laughter we find release and a new perspective on life. Our leisure time must be used as in the sight of God. All too few of us plan creatively what to do with the free time at our disposal. When we say we are killing time, we are committing spiritual suicide. A Christian should give time to serious reading, devoting some part of each day to a study of the Bible and then of the best books, for one is called upon to love God with the mind.

There must be time for worship, both public and private. Being a member of a church means more than attending public worship though it certainly does mean that and all that it involves. "Oliver Wendell Holmes once said that there was in the corner of his heart a plant called reverence which needed watering about once a week."[4] We have in our hearts a whole garden which needs watering each week, namely the flowers of faith, hope, love, and forgiveness. These flowers become droopy at times and need reviving, and this our Sunday worship can do for us. But Sunday worship needs supplementing by private prayer. We need to make time for prayer.

Our churches are suffering from the lack of helpers—teachers in the church school, singers in the choir, workers to visit the sick and the lonely and the unchurched and to carry on the social and educational enterprises which are needed if the church is to thrive. All about us are fields white unto harvest but the laborers are few. Are we willing to use some of our God-given time in the service of Christ and his church?

To use time well, we have to make up our minds that there is not time for everything. But we are in the driver's seat, and we can choose whether time is to be a tyrant or a servant. We must make sure that what we choose to do with our time will stand the scrutiny of God's

TIME—TYRANT OR SERVANT? • 69

judgment. Paul said to the Corinthians, "The time is short" (1 Corinthians 7:29). The fact that time ends for each of us gives it its impressive meaning and moves us to redeem the time, to buy up the opportunity. Time is sacred because God hallowed it by the redemptive work of Christ. His birth, life, death, and resurrection took place in time and are so identified with it that Paul could declare: "Behold, now is the accepted time; behold, now is the day of salvation" (2 Corinthians 6:2). Life is too short to lose opportunities. It is only a redeemed life which can redeem time.

Think how Christ used his time on earth, unhurried, unresting. He said, "Are there not twelve hours in the day?" (John 11:9). "I must work the works of him that sent me, while it is day: the night cometh, when no man can work" (John 9:4). It is always very wonderful to me that Christ felt the shortness of time. Most of us are afraid to look time in the face, but Christ was not. He knew that if God had given him a twelve-hour work, God would give him the twelve hours in which to do it. That was the faith of Paul as well. To every time its task and to every task its time. Jesus and Paul could say with the psalmist, "My times are in thy hand" (Psalm 31:15). Time is God's servant carrying us onward to him. Is time for you a tyrant or is it God's servant working on your behalf? If we believe that we are accountable to God, that our time comes from him, and that in time we are fitting ourselves to step into his presence, then we shall have a new respect for the days God has given us.

There are three inscriptions on the door of the Milan Cathedral. Over the right-hand portal is a sculptured wreath of flowers with the words, "All that pleases is but for a moment." Over the left-hand entrance are a cross and a crown under which are the words, "All that troubles is but for a moment." Over the central door is a simple sentence, "Nothing is important save that which is eternal." Time is a fragment of eternity. God, who is beyond time, has given time to us as a solemn stewardship. So we must make the most of the time that is ours.

The very swiftness of the course of time makes our restless hearts cry out for the timeless. The very changefulness of time makes us feel our need of a shelter that shall never crumble. The uncertainties of time drive us closer to him who has been the refuge of his people in all generations—"thou, O Lord, art our father, our redeemer; thy name is from everlasting" (Isaiah 63:16). Time has done its best for us when it has led us into his fellowship as into the light of a sun that does not

70 • COURAGE TO LIVE

go down. Time cannot do its worst for us if it leaves us at the feet of the One who is the same yesterday, today, and forever. The highest service time can render us is to introduce us to the timeless One and to give us the opportunity of working out in the life of the world his eternal will.

9

Hindrances to Prayer

"That your prayers be not hindered." 1 Peter 3:7

The effect of prayer on the spirit is so wonderful, the transformation of fear and worry into calm and confidence, that one can say of it with Dr. Fosdick: "If there is any element in human life to whose inestimable value we have abundant testimony, it is prayer; and to leave misunderstood and untrained a power capable of such high uses is a spiritual tragedy." [1] Yet there are many Christians who leave this power practically unexercised. They may use a form of words in the morning or at the close of day, but how few pray in the proper sense of the word, that is, pray in the Holy Spirit! Why is this? Must it not be because many do not believe in the power of prayer? If they believed that such a mighty weapon lay close to their hand, they would surely use it more. Why do they not believe it? Possibly because they have ceased to get any good from it. A woman once said to me, "I have given up praying. There's no good in it." She was suffering from an incurable disease, and because the answer did not come, she had

71

72 • COURAGE TO LIVE

given up praying. It is probable that she had never known what spiritual prayer was. She had used it only for material benefits. Her case is not unusual. There are thousands of prayers that go up to God and get no answer at all, because they never reach him. Something hinders their approach to him. Let us consider some of the difficulties and disappointments of the inner life. One of the chief of these is that of unanswered prayer.

It is interesting to notice how Peter brings it before us in a curious, unexpected way. He is addressing Christian husbands, and he tells them to be kind to their wives as to the weaker vessel and as fellow-heirs of the grace of God. Then he goes on to speak of the results of such a home life. One might expect him to add "that your home life may be happy" or "that you may be an example to your heathen neighbors." But it is something quite different. It is: "that your prayers be not hindered" (1 Peter 3:7).

What does he mean by that? Surely this—that unless our prayers come from a worthy heart, they will not have power with God. If the telephone wire is cut, a man may shout his loudest, but nothing will get through. Sin cuts the wire between the soul and God. Shakespeare in the prayer scene in *Hamlet* has given us a picture of such a soul. The wicked king wants to be pardoned by God, but only on the condition that he "retain the offence." He says:

> My words fly up, my thoughts remain below:
> Words without thoughts never to heaven go.[2]

This, says Isaiah, was the reason God did not listen to Israel's prayers. "When ye spread forth your hands, I will hide mine eyes from you: yea, when ye make many prayers, I will not hear you." Why? "Your hands are full of blood" (Isaiah 1:15). All the week they were oppressing the widows and the fatherless, and so God could not listen to their prayers.

"Ask and ye shall receive," says our Lord, but the asking to which he refers is something more than verbal petition. It is a quest with the whole being. Before we receive what we ask, there is a price to be paid. The reason for so much unanswered prayer is that we are not willing to pay the price. The blessings can be given only to those who are worthy and ready to receive them. James and John prayed that, when Jesus came into his kingdom, they might have the places of honor at his right hand and his left. His reply was: "Ye know not what ye ask. Are ye able to drink of the cup that I shall drink of?" (Matthew 20:22).

HINDRANCES TO PRAYER • 73

If they could have looked into the future and could have seen Jesus on his cross with a cross on either side, would they still have prayed that prayer?

It would be very unreasonable to give up praying because some prayer of ours has not been answered in the way we hoped. How unfitted we are to substitute our will for God's will! As Longfellow once wrote: "What discord should we bring into the universe if our prayers were all answered! Then *we* should govern the world and not God. And do you think we should govern it better?"[3] Have you ever thought of the dangers of answered prayer? There is a passage in one of the psalms which refers to the Israelites wandering in the wilderness. "They soon forgat his works; they waited not for his counsel . . .[but] tempted God in the desert. And he gave them their request; but sent leanness into their soul" (Psalm 106:13-15).

It is not good for us to get all we want. We may set our hearts on the wrong things. We may ask for things which it would not be good for us to have. If we look deep enough, we will find God's guiding hand in failure and disappointment. God's way is the only way of true fulfillment. The Bible is full of unanswered prayers. Moses prayed to enter the Promised Land but died on Mount Nebo, his request refused. Job complained to God: "I cry unto thee, and thou dost not hear me" (Job 30:20). The prophet Habakkuk said: "O Lord, how long shall I cry, and thou wilt not hear!" (Habakkuk 1:2). Paul prayed three times that his thorn in the flesh might be removed, but for the rest of his life he was compelled to bear it. Even our Lord in Gethsemane prayed that he might not have to drink the cup, but He went out to drain it to the very dregs.

We must learn to recognize that "No" is as real an answer to prayer as "Yes." When we consider how partial is our knowledge and how narrow is our outlook, we can understand that God must often have to say to us, "Ye know not what ye ask." A little boy prayed for a fine day for an outing, but when the day came, it poured with rain. His mother said, "You see, God didn't answer your prayer." The boy, wiser than she, replied, "Oh, yes, he did. He said 'No.'" Some prayers must be denied because of their character. This is a point which the Bible emphasizes when it says: "You ask and do not receive, because you ask wrongly" (James 4:33, RSV). God loves us far too much to give us all that we ask. Sometimes the form of our petition may be denied in order that God may give us the substance of our desire. St. Augustine pictures his mother, Monica, praying all night in a wayside

74 • COURAGE TO LIVE

chapel on the coast of North Africa that God would not let her son sail for Italy. She wanted him to become a Christian, and she was afraid for him if he went to Italy with its many temptations and was away from her influence. But even while she prayed for her son to remain at home, he sailed for Italy. There, under the influence of Bishop Ambrose, he became a Christian in the very place from which his mother's prayers would have kept him. So Augustine says: "Thou, in the depth of thy counsels, hearing the main point of her desire, regardedst not what she *then asked,* that Thou mightest make me what she *ever desired."*[4]

Many of our prayers must be denied because we utter them in ignorance of the needs of others and the consequences if our desires were granted. Sometimes our prayers are of such a kind that to answer them God would have to be cruel, unjust, or irresponsible, that is, he would cease to be God. We may be praying for something which would benefit us and at the same time hurt others. Here is an illustration of this. An important express train was due to leave a London terminal. An agitated lady approached the stationmaster and begged him to postpone the departure of the train. He told her that the only person who had power to do that was the General Manager. She rushed to his office and repeated her request. She said, "We have just heard that our boy has met with a serious accident and is not expected to live. My husband is on his way, but he can't possibly arrive until fifteen minutes after the departure of the train. If you hold up the train, you will be giving him the only chance of seeing the boy alive. If you have any spark of human sympathy, you will not refuse." The General Manager said, "I am very sorry for you and your husband, but I can't do it. This train makes more than one important connection which would be lost if I delayed the train. There may be others to whom the catching of one of those connections may mean as much as to your husband. My business is to serve the community by maintaining the most trustworthy service possible."[5]

It would be a sorry world for all of us if some of our unwise petitions did not have "No" for their answers. We do not always know what is best for us or for those for whom we pray. We want things that may not be for their highest good or ours. We say "Give me" far more frequently than we say "Make me" or "Use me." Look back over your life. Have you not reason to be thankful that some of your prayers were denied?

Some of our petitions are refused because we are not willing to help

HINDRANCES TO PRAYER • 75

God answer them. A few years ago a student in deep distress called to see me. He blurted out that he no longer believed that God answered prayer. When I asked him his reason for that conclusion, he told me God had let him down in an examination. I found that he had been making prayer a substitute for work, and when it did not yield the expected result, he blamed God. We may smile at that student, but how often we repeat his mistake! How many of us pray that others may be led to Christ but we never do anything to help God answer our prayers? We never put ourselves into God's hands to speak a word of witness for him or to invite our friend to a place where God will be able to reach him. The result is that our prayers are not answered. We ourselves are the stumbling block.

There is still another reason why our petitions may be refused and that is that we are not always ready to receive the gifts we desire. If God is good and loving and knows all our needs and wants to give us the best, we ask, "Why should it be necessary to ask him for anything? Why cannot he give us all the things we need at once?" The reason is that God can give only as we are able to receive. It is in order that he may be able to give that God requires us to ask. God is always more ready to hear than we are to pray and is wont to give us more than we desire or deserve.

That is why Jesus was so insistent on tireless prayer. The way to get your prayers answered, if they are worthy, is to make yourself a nuisance. There is a persistence that gets through. A little boy who badly wanted a watch and meant to get it pestered every member of the family until he was forbidden to mention the word "watch" under threat of dire punishment. He was sent off to learn a text before he went to bed. In due course he returned to recite his chosen text to the assembled family. It was this: "And what I say unto you I say unto all, Watch." He got it, though it was only a cheap one. Importunity does count. It is a sign of earnestness. "Men ought always to pray and not to faint," said Jesus, and he went on to tell the parable of the importunate widow and the judge, who finally dealt with her case, "lest she wear me out with her continual coming" (see Luke 18:1-8). He also illustrated prayer by the story of the friend who came at midnight and who because of his persistence gained his request for help.

Margaret Blair Johnstone, a Congregationalist minister, in her autobiography entitled *When God Says No,* with the subtitle "Faith's Starting Point," speaks of three talismans which have meant much to

76 • COURAGE TO LIVE

her: "Hold on; don't run; one step more." She says that sometimes people lose faith in God when the answer to their prayer is "No," but that is precisely when he hopes most that we find him. "Only when God says 'No' do we ever measure what we want against what He wants for us. Only when we dare to answer as Jesus did, 'Not my will but Thine be done,' do we grow toward our best selves, towards one another and towards Him."[6]

There is another answer that God often gives to our prayers besides "Yes" and "No." It is "Wait." Christ warned us that even when our requests are granted, they will not always be granted at once. We have to learn to wait patiently for God's time. Prayer is often a slow process rather than a swift action. It is a protracted campaign rather than a single operation. Boys ring doorbells and run away. So many of us pray. But anyone who has serious business will wait for an answer to his or her summons and, if need be, will ring again. Such patient waiting is the test of our earnestness. Often God gives us something quite different in answer and far better than we had asked for. Prayer is not an attempt to persuade God to do what he had not intended to do. It is a method of liberating the hand of God to do what he wants to do but cannot do, unless we cooperate with him.

Many of us have cause to thank God for the prayers that he has answered, but some of us have had more cause to thank him for the prayers he has not answered, or rather, for the higher answers he has given to our short-sighted prayers. God himself is better than all his gifts, and sometimes his hand has to come to us empty in order that he may grasp us and lift us up to a higher level of thought and feeling.

When God cannot answer our petitions, he can answer us. Think of Paul's experience. "There was given to me a thorn in the flesh, the messenger of Satan to buffet me, lest I should be exalted above measure. . . . I besought the Lord thrice, that it might depart from me. And he said unto me, My grace is sufficient for thee: for my strength is made perfect in weakness" (2 Corinthians 12:7-9). Paul asked for the removal of his physical limitation, and instead he received the power to triumph over it. His prayer for relief was not answered, but he was answered with a reply that put fresh courage into him. He was not healed, but he was helped. By the help of God's grace he was able to live with his disability and so became more compassionate toward his fellowmen.

An amazing statement was made at the end of his life by the first missionary to Burma, Adoniram Judson: "I never prayed sincerely

HINDRANCES TO PRAYER • 77

and earnestly for anything, but it came; at some time—no matter at how distant a day—somehow, in some shape—probably the last I should have devised—it came."[7] All his prayers were answered. But consider his story. He prayed to go to India but was sent to Burma. He prayed for his wife's life to be spared, but he had to bury her and two of his children. He prayed for release from the prison into which the King of Ava had thrust him, but he had to lie there for many months. Many of his most urgent petitions were unanswered, but Judson himself was mightily answered. Unforeseen doors were opened through the very trials he had sought to avoid.

It was so with our Lord himself. "Let this cup pass" was a prayer that could not be answered, but Jesus himself was wonderfully answered in the garden. He went out from there to face his judges and accusers and the cross itself with a calm that no suffering could shake. He went into Gethsemane in the dark; he came out in the light because he had talked with God. He went into Gethsemane in an agony; he came out with victory won and with peace in his soul, because he had talked with God.

God must answer prayer. There is no God if prayer is not answered. If there were one unanswered prayer, then God would cease to be God, for he would have missed an opportunity of expressing his love. Every prayer is answered in some way. The answer may be "Yes" or "No" or "Wait." It may be delayed or not recognized. God does not always respond in the way we expect. He responds with the best when we have only asked for the second best. But every prayer is answered in God's way, and one day we shall discover that his way is better than ours.

Let us consider some practical difficulties which perplex many who sincerely try to pray. One is a sense of unreality, a lack of a vivid awareness of God when we pray. This may be due to the lack of a true perspective of spirit as we come into God's presence through want of time or the absorption of our minds with worldly pursuits. Unreality is often due to some unconfessed sin or to some part of life not yet surrendered to God. The psalmist writes: "If I regard iniquity in my heart, the Lord will not hear me" (Psalm 66:18). Jesus said to his disciples, "If you do not forgive men their trespasses, neither will your Father forgive your trespasses" (Mathew 6:15, RSV). In the Scriptures the two most formidable hindrances to prayer are impurity of thought and the unforgiving spirit. Total surrender to God is also a condition of seeing his face.

78 • COURAGE TO LIVE

We cannot always pray with the same intensity and satisfaction. But we must not give way to moods. A man does not deny the existence of the sun because it is a cloudy day. Moods are the clouds in our spiritual skies; we must not on account of them cease to trust the God whom for the time being they obscure. Keep up the form of prayer even though at times it seems as if there were no God to hear. When you cannot pray as you would like, pray as you can.

It is unwise to refuse to pray unless we feel in the mood for it, for then the inclination to pray will come less and less frequently until we give up prayer altogether. More than one saint has told us that it is not until we are feeling utterly bored with our prayers and still continue to pray that we can know the power and the joy of prayer. God does not want us any the less because we do not feel like coming to him in prayer. If we have an appointment with a friend at a certain hour, we keep it, however disinclined we may feel when the time comes. Are we to be less courteous with our heavenly Friend? God often does far more for us when we pray against our inclination than when we pray with it. The very submission of our will deepens our surrender.

Faith and not feeling determines the effectiveness of our prayers. Let your feelings take care of themselves. Let your prayers be sheer acts of duty, regular and punctual, and the intention will be well pleasing to God. Prayer is not a matter of feelings but of the will, and if our will is set toward God, all will be well. All may not be easy, but all is well. I remember hearing Dom Bernard Clements say in a broadcast talk on prayer:

> Lest we should grow to depend too much on our feelings, God takes them away, as our mother took away her hand when we were learning to walk. So we must go forward and in that way our will will grow. When the darkness comes and we begin to feel unreality in our prayers, we are like little children moved from one class to another and we find the lessons difficult and are inclined to give up. But if we persevere, we shall attain a strength and certainty which nothing can shake.[8]

Another difficulty we all find in prayer is concentration. We are prey to wandering thoughts. Our minds wander so much that we are tempted to give up the effort altogether. One way of dealing with such wandering thoughts is to take them as they come and draw them in and make them a subject of prayer. Some interview we have before us or some person with whom we have had a difference keeps flashing into our minds as we try to pray. Instead of struggling to dismiss the

HINDRANCES TO PRAYER • 79

thoughts, start praying about them. Weave distractions into prayers, and they are suddenly transformed from hindrances into helps. Instead of drawing the mind away, they give it new content. A woman told me recently of the joy that filled her life when she made this discovery. For years she had tried to discipline her mind until the thought of prayer became a nightmare. Then somebody suggested turning the enemy into a friend. It has revolutionized her prayer life. Not only are her prayers more comprehensive, but also since she adopted this new attitude to wandering thoughts, she has not had half as many as before.

It is not always possible to do this. So let the thoughts come in and out but do not attend to them. We shall be conscious of them, of course, for we are always conscious of quite a number of things besides the one we are attending to. But we shall not give them our attention, for that is fixed on our prayer.

Prayer costs persistence in the face of difficulties. As the German hymn-writer, Gerhard Tersteegen, says:

> Yet hindrances strew all the way;
> I aim at Thee, yet from Thee stray.[9]

The unreality of God, the difficulty of holding the mind to the act of prayer, the wayward mood, and the wandering thought—all these are hindrances that men of prayer have known. A famous Oxford scholar of the last century, Benjamin Jowett, the Master of Balliol, wrote this in his diary:

> Nothing makes one more conscious of poverty and shallowness of character than difficulty in praying or attending to prayer. Any thoughts about self, thoughts of evil, daydreams, love fancies, easily find an abode in the mind. But the thought of God and of right and truth will not stay there. ... There is nothing which ... I seem to desire more than the knowledge of God ... and yet for two minutes I cannot keep my mind upon [him]. But I read a great work of fiction and can hardly take my mind from it. If I had any real love of God, would not my mind dwell upon him?[10]

There is one other hindrance to prayer I wish to mention, and that is too much stress on speaking. We suppose that no prayer is being offered unless we are talking all the time. But our Lord told us that we shall not be heard for our much speaking. Some would change the line of the hymn from "Master, speak, Thy servant heareth" to "Master, listen, for Thy servant speaketh." They seem to know nothing of silent adoration or quiet waiting upon God. There are times when speech is easy and when one can pour out the heart in a

80 • COURAGE TO LIVE

torrent of words, with all the natural simplicity of a child talking to his father. But there are other times when we cannot find words to express our desires: grief or disappointment or sin strike us dumb. Then we must listen for the still, small voice that speaks within, and offer a prayer like this of Charles Wesley:

> From the world of sin, and noise,
> And hurry I withdraw;
> For the small and inward voice
> I wait with humble awe;
> Silent am I now and still,
> Dare not in Thy presence move;
> To my waiting soul reveal
> The secret of Thy love. [11]

In the story of the life of that great French saint of the last century, the Curé of Ars, we read of one of his peasants who used to remain for hours on his knees before the altar in the church, without even moving his lips. One day the Curé asked him, "What do you say to our Lord?" The old peasant replied, "I say nothing to Him. I just sit and take counsel with Him and He takes counsel with me." [12] The greatest of the saints have found no formula at once so simple, so exact, so sublime, and so complete as this to express the conversation of the soul with God. In such a communion all our problems about prayer and all hindrances and difficulties in the inner life seem to disappear. In his will we find our peace. God himself is better than all his gifts.

10

Burdens and How to Bear Them

"Every man shall bear his own burden"—Galatians 6:5
"Bear ye one another's burdens"—Galatians 6:2
"Cast thy burden upon the Lord"—Psalm 55:22

There are many people who are unable to live to the fullest because the burdens of life keep them down. It is not the physical load they carry that breaks them but the inner load of conflicts and fears and anxieties. The burdens are not always visible because most people do not like to advertise their troubles. But if you look into their faces, you will see the lines of anxiety, and in their shoulders you will see signs of strain. There must be some way to bear the burden, to handle the load of life. I have been caught in several storms while flying, and I will admit that I am never quite at ease when the plane is being tossed about in the sky. But the one thought that offers me assurance in the storm is that the engineers who designed the plane knew that such storms would be encountered. They took them into account and built into the plane the strength to withstand the storms. Surely God has done the same in his creation. He knows all about the turbulent pressures, the inner burdens which we have to bear, and he has planned us to be equal to the task.

82 • COURAGE TO LIVE

The Bible has a great deal to say on the subject of burdens, because it is a practical book, and it knows exactly what our lives are. There is no better way of summarizing its teaching on burdens than by putting together the three sentences which are at the head of this chapter. There are burdens which no one can share with us, which we must carry alone, and of these, save in the presence of God, it is best to be silent. "Every man shall bear his own burden." This statement emphasizes the need for personal fortitude and courage, something which we can only give to ourselves. There are other burdens which those who love us are sharing with us every day. "Bear ye one another's burdens." This statement reminds us that we need the sympathy and encouragement of others. Whatever our burdens may be, whether they are our own or of one close to us, whether they are secret or public, God sustains us in the bearing of them. He himself bears them with us. "Cast thy burden upon the Lord." This statement reminds us of the inspiration of our faith, the strength which can come only from God.

"Every man shall bear his own burden." The Greek word which Paul uses for "burden" is the same word which is used to describe a ship's cargo. Everyone must bear his or her own cargo of responsibility. All of us have to make our own decisions, choose our own paths, live our own lives. We must travel alone. No one can walk with us save for a little way. Each one has a burden which must be carried as a soldier carries his pack. There is a burden appointed, just as there is a warfare appointed, from which there is no discharge. There are burdens visible and invisible: burdens of the body, sickness and pain; burdens of the mind, anxiety about ourselves and our loved ones; burdens of the heart, sorrow, disappointment, wounded affection; burdens of the soul, the burden of temptation which is laid upon us all, and the burden of sin.

There is no clue to the mystery of life unless you believe that in this world we are in a school of training. We are being trained by God to fulfill his purpose, and at last, having been fully trained, we shall share eternal life with him. That is why God says to us, "Carry your own pack." There is no way of avoiding it. The good mother tries everything within her power to comfort her child in pain and to relieve its suffering, but the pain is something which the child alone must bear. It is the same with making a decision. Others may warn and instruct you, put their experience at your disposal, but a time comes when you have to determine which way to go. It is the same

BURDENS AND HOW TO BEAR THEM • 83

thing in the most sacred relationship of your soul with God. No one can occupy the place in the heart of God which, from all eternity, he has appointed for you.

We cannot escape this sense of responsibility for our lives. Willing or unwilling, we all must bear our own burdens. In one of his poems Schiller tells how when God first made the birds, they had beautiful plumage and sweet voices but no wings. Then God laid their wings on the ground and said, "Take these burdens and bear them." The birds said, "Burdens! Oh, how dreadful! Still, we will carry them as bravely as we can." The burdens they took up began to grow to them and spread out and helped them to fly. Without those burdens they could never have risen from the ground. Quite often our burdens turn out to be wings. Thomas Edison, who improved the telephone, was very deaf. When someone spoke of the handicap this must be in his work, he replied that it had turned out to be a blessing because it led him to discover a receiver so perfect that he could hear it himself. We speak of the burden of poverty, and often it is a sad burden. But sometimes the boy who is born poor has had to work so hard that he has developed a strong and noble character and in the end stood out among his fellows in a way he might never have done but for his early struggles. When burdens are laid upon us, we sometimes exclaim, "How dreadful!" But when we take them up and bear them cheerfully, the burdens turn into wings, raising us up to be better men and women and lifting us nearer to God. "Every man shall bear his own burden." That is the way in which God disciplines our souls and develops our lives and makes them strong.

The hallmark of our maturity is a sense of responsibility for ourselves and the deeds done in the body. The hallmark of the Christian is a sense of responsibility for others: "Bear ye one another's burdens." The Greek word here translated "burden" means literally something that presses on a person. The word is found in ancient records for a burden of oppression or a burden of taxation. It is used about the exhausted condition of the laborers in the vineyard who bore the heat and burden of the day. Paul uses the same word in his letter to the Romans. "We then that are strong ought to bear the infirmities of the weak" (Romans 15:1). When he wrote to his young disciple Timothy, he said, ". . . endure hardness as a good soldier of Jesus Christ" (2 Timothy 2:3). It is up to all of us to put into life at least as much as we take out. In every age Christianity has produced an elect company of men and women who have felt a responsibility

84 • COURAGE TO LIVE

for others. They have carried the burden of the world on their own hearts, bearing in their bodies the marks of the Lord Jesus.

I think of Josephine Butler, that sensitive and cultured woman, who was called quite early in life to learn that suffering may be the means of making possible a new growth of the soul. One night she and her husband returned home from the Continent. Their excited little daughter rushing to greet them lost her balance on the stairs, fell to the bottom, and was killed instantly. "Never can I lose that memory," she said, "the fall, the sudden cry, and then the silence. Would God I had died that death for her." To her in her sorrow came an old Quaker lady who said, "I have spent most of my life looking after girls taken from the streets. I am old now and and can no longer handle the work of looking after the home where forty of them live. Come and take my job, and you will forget your own sorrow."[1] Josephine Butler went; and by taking on her shoulders the burdens of others, she found her own burden bearable.

You cannot think of others as she did until self is completely forgotten. There may not be much you can do to help your friends and neighbors to bear their burdens, but you can pray for them. Do not leave that little bit undone. To know that we care may make all the difference. Some comfort given, some kindness shown by us, may well put them on their feet and lead them to the God of all comfort in whose strength all burdens must be borne. We all have our own burdens and often it seems as if they are enough to carry. But Paul says, in effect, "Take another and balance your own." Every life is either diminishing or adding to the burdens of other lives. When we help another bear his or her burden, we act like the great Burdenbearer himself. We fulfill the law of Christ.

Dr. W. Russell Maltby tells a story of a man in a position of trust who was found guilty of shameful conduct, dismissed from his post, and his disgrace made public. As so often happens, the burden of it fell most heavily on his relatives. One of them was his daughter who had made a place for herself in society and was much looked up to and admired. But when one of her friends said to her, "It is terrible that you should be involved in his disgrace and your name dragged in the mud," she replied indignantly, "When I heard of it, I said, 'Well, thank God I can share it.'"[2] Real love desires to share the burden of the beloved.

What a different world we should have if all were to attempt to fulfill the law of Christ and bear one another's burdens! The Jews

BURDENS AND HOW TO BEAR THEM • 85

have a beautiful legend about the building of the temple. On the temple site two brothers had adjoining farms. One brother was married and had children; the other was unmarried. When harvest time came around, the married brother said to himself, "My brother has no wife or children and lives a lonely life. I will cheer his heart by taking some of my sheaves and adding them to his." The other brother said to himself, "My brother has a wife and many children. I will help him by taking some of my sheaves and adding them to his." Thus it was that each morning each brother's stock of sheaves rose higher and both of them wondered how it happened. At length the mystery was solved. One night, as the harvest moon was shining, the two brothers met one another, each with his arms full of sheaves and bound for his brother's field. There where they met one another that night, according to the legend, rose the temple of God. As Charles Wesley bids us, we should pray:

Help us to help each other, Lord,
Each other's cross to bear;
Let each his friendly aid afford,
And feel his brother's care.[3]

There is a disturbing parable in the story John M. Wilson tells of the glowworms in Maitoma Cave in New Zealand. The cave is inhabited by a galaxy of tiny glowworms that attach themselves to the roof and walls of the cave. They are busy fishing for insect food. As they fish, their lights shine. The hungrier the glowworm, the brighter is his light. He spins and lets down fine threads from the roof of the cave. When a gnat or some other small insect, attracted by the light, collides with one of these strange fishing lines, it is caught and held. The glowworm reels in the line and consumes the captive. When its hunger is satisfied, the glowworm puts out its light. The soft lights that give the Glowworm Grotto its unearthly light are not produced by contented glowworms but by glowworms that are hungry and in dead earnest about their fishing. With us, as with the glowworms, comfort too often brings complacency. Satisfied and comfortable, our lights go out, and we ignore the needs of those who still are hungry or hurt or in despair. Intent upon remaining comfortable, we resent the struggles of the uncomfortable and accept all too little responsibility for their needs. But the Christian faith rightly insists that society cannot be free unless it becomes a community of the socially concerned. We are all bound in the bundle of life together.

86 • COURAGE TO LIVE

Were Paul alive today, he would surely regard many of the social changes of this century as fulfillment of this principle of bearing one another's burdens. The social conscience has been awakened. All the wealth of social services are a highly complex way of sharing the burdens that have to be borne. Modern society is an elaborate system of mutual aid. We need to hear the challenge to become more eager to minister than to be ministered unto. We read in Exodus that when Moses was grown, he went out unto his brethren and looked on their burdens. Are we sufficiently grown to do that? In the Middle East, in Southeast Asia, in India, and in Latin America are hungry, ill-clad brothers and sisters of ours. Can we see them? Can we see the burdens of those who are being strangled by hunger, disease, and despair? Do we agree with William Blake when he says:

> Can I see another's woe,
> And not be in sorrow too?
> Can I see another's grief,
> And not seek for kind relief?[4]

Christians are called to go out to their brethren and see their burdens and do something about them. They are called to bear the burdens of all unprivileged people—the millions who are illiterate and superstitious; the displaced persons who are helpless refugees, victims of war; the oppressed black people; the weak-willed victims of gambling, drugs, and drink; the lonely sick; the feeble; the aged; and the juvenile delinquents.

If we are to do this, we must look for help to Christ who had compassion on the multitude. He identified himself completely with all who labor and are heavy-laden, and in him as in no other they found and still find rest. He gets beneath the burden by carrying the cross. In Marc Connelly's play, *Green Pastures,* in the final scene Gabriel listens to God as He tells him something about what the boy told him, something about Hosea and himself and how they found something. Gabriel asks, "What, Lawd?" "Mercy, through *sufferin',"* God replied. "Yes, Lawd," Gabriel says. "I'm trying to find it too! . . ." "It's awful impo'tant to all de people on my earth," God says. "Did he mean dat even God must suffer?" Gabriel asks.

Then in the distance are heard cries, "Oh, look at Him! Oh, look, dey goin' to make him carry it up dat high hill! Dey goin' to nail him to it! Oh, dat's a terrible burden for one man to carry!"[5] God himself in the Son of his love joins his children, the little brothers of his Son, and bears their burdens in the terrible burden of the cross.

Many people today think of religion as a restraint rather than an inspiration, a burden rather than a bridge, something that they have to carry rather than something that can carry them. To John Bunyan, coming to Christ meant, first of all, deliverance from a burden that had grown unbearable; so in *Pilgrim's Progress* he makes Christian's burden roll away out of sight at the foot of the cross.

We must all travel alone; yet we are not alone, for the Father is with us. He will keep us from falling. God is too wise a Father to seek to remove his child's individual responsibility. He is too true a Father to leave his child lonely and helpless. We may not put our burdens on others, but we may cast them upon God. He knows us personally. He can bear our burdens. They would crush our neighbor, but they will not crush God. He can bear them as easily as the Atlantic bears a bubble or Mount Everest a snowflake.

Burdens are just as varied as blessings. They may be private or public, real or imaginary. But once we have learned the lesson that God is with us and will see us through, then we are set free from anxious care. When we cast our burdens on the Lord, he does not always take them away. Sometimes he does, but more often he does not; but the promise is that when we cast our burdens on the Lord, he will sustain us. He will make us adequate to the burden. Whatever our burdens may be, God can take them away or enable us to bear them without distress.

There is a story in the life of Hudson Taylor, the founder of the China Inland Mission, which has often helped me. On one occasion while he was talking to a young member of the mission, letters came in with news of serious rioting in one of the mission stations and of grave dangers to the lives of the missionaries. George Nichol was about to slip out and leave Taylor alone, when to his astonishment he heard him begin to whistle. "How *can* you whistle, when our friends are in such danger!" he asked. "Would you have me anxious and troubled?" was Taylor's quiet reply. "That would not help them, and would certainly incapacitate me for my work. I have just to roll the burden on the Lord."[6] What he had been whistling was the refrain of a hymn, "Jesus, I am resting, resting, in the joy of what Thou art."

Many of us are carrying heavy burdens, and at times the loneliness of it will strike terror in our hearts. But in fellowship with others we shall find the burdens lifted a little especially if we seek to ease another's burden. Bishop William A. Quayle, an American Methodist bishop, once described how he had faced a problem one

88 • COURAGE TO LIVE

night that seemed too hard to solve. He prayed, but his prayers seemed to get nowhere. He lay on his bed and tossed about, unable to sleep. Then about midnight God spoke to him and said, "Quayle, you go to bed, I'll sit up the rest of the night."[7] What a difference it makes to know that we are not alone, that we are not left to struggle on alone as best we may! There is always Someone else there. When it is you and God together, you can face anything.

11

The Conquest of Suffering

"... the whole creation groaneth and travaileth in pain together until now." Romans 8:22

There have been many statements about the pain that is in the world, but in this verse the apostle Paul sums up the whole age-long agony in one short sentence. Pain is universal. It runs everywhere through creation, and the result is widespread misery. We have only to open our eyes to see it. Pain is one of the saddest facts in human experience, and nothing is gained by attempting to deny it.

We are more sensitive to the presence of pain than our forebears seem to have been. We pay more attention to its existence, and our sympathies are more readily aroused. One striking difference between the ancient world and ours is the absence then of all institutions for the care of the sick, the disabled, and the unfortunate. Hospitals, orphanages, and old people's homes are the products of Christian civilization. The tenderness toward suffering in the world today is the result of the transforming work of Jesus. A new sympathy

90 • COURAGE TO LIVE

has come into the world's outlook on pain because of One who went about healing the sick.

"Why should this happen to me?" is the very natural question which we ask about our own suffering or that of a loved one. Throughout my ministry this problem has pressed upon my mind. In one church after another it has seemed as if the most valuable members have been struck down while others who did little but criticize were able to boast that they had never had a day's illness in their lives. We must try to find an answer to this question, for it deeply troubles many minds and sometimes disturbs or even shatters people's faith. How often I have heard someone say, "I can't understand why this thing should have been allowed to happen" or "He was a good man and did not deserve to have such pain" or "I prayed and prayed for her recovery, but she died." It is probable that more people lose faith in God because of this problem of suffering than through any other cause.

Studdart Kennedy once remarked that a man who was undisturbed by the problem of pain was suffering from one of two things—either from a hardening of the heart or a softening of the brain. Everyone who is mentally alive, especially one who believes in a God of love, finds this problem difficult to solve. If God is our heavenly Father, as Christ declares he is, why does he permit all this suffering? Could he not stop it? Or does he not want to stop it? If we cannot bear to hear the groaning and travailing of the world in its pain, how can he bear it? As a sorrowing father said to me after he had been watching by the deathbed of his daughter, "Had it been in my power to bear her pain for her, how gladly would I have done it! I could not bear to see her suffer; how is it that God could?" A mother stands at the bedside of an only child stricken with polio and asks, "Why?" A husband watches his wife grow weaker day by day from the ravages of cancer and asks, "Why?" A young father dies of a heart attack, leaving behind two small children, and the widow asks, "Why?" Wars bring unmeasured suffering, and humanity asks, "Why?"

The first and easiest explanation of suffering is that it comes as a punishment for wrongdoing. This does happen. If I sin against common sense and put my hand in a fire, it will be burned. If I sin against the laws of health, I will be punished by sickness and disease. It is sin and folly and ignorance and selfishness which are responsible for a vast amount of suffering. All sin involves suffering, but it is not true to say that all suffering is due to sin. Again and again in the

THE CONQUEST OF SUFFERING • 91

course of my ministry I have met good people who, if some suffering comes upon them, ask, "What have I done that this has happened to me?" Job insisted that he had done nothing to deserve his suffering, but his friends said over and over again that he must have sinned or that suffering would never have come upon him. But Job refused to accept this explanation and finally reached a deeper and true answer to his problem.

In the Gospel of Luke we read of some people who told Jesus about the Galileans whose blood Pilate mingled with their sacrifices. He said to them: "Suppose ye that these Galileans were sinners above all the Galileans, because they suffered such things? I tell you, Nay" (Luke 13:2-3a). So we have the authority of Jesus to assure us that not all suffering is the result of sin. There was a day, which John records in his Gospel, when Jesus met the man who had been blind from birth. "And his disciples asked him, saying, Master, who did sin, this man, or his parents, that he was born blind? Jesus answered, Neither hath this man sinned, nor his parents" (John 9:2-3a).

A second explanation of the fact of pain and suffering is that it may be a discipline. Pain may be one of the supreme safeguards of life. If fire did not hurt, we might all have been burned up long ago. Pain often gives timely warning of disease which, without it, would soon prove fatal. There is need for danger signals which the pain fibers in our nerves are designed to transmit. Pain points the doctor to the spot where the peril is, and the kind of pain often tells the doctor where the peril is. If you have no pain, the doctor will probe and press you until the pain is found so that treatment can begin. Pain is not the destroyer but the preserver of the body. Pain insists upon being attended to. As C. S. Lewis says in his book, *The Problem of Pain:* "God whispers to us in our pleasures, speaks in our conscience but shouts in our pains: it is His megaphone to rouse a deaf world." [1]

It is a curious fact that among all living things man appears to possess the highest capacity for suffering. The higher creatures stand in the scale of life, the more they are susceptible to pain. The more highly developed the nervous system, the more sensitive it is. Our power of imagination multiplies our suffering. It is not the pain that matters most but our reaction to it. Merely to endure our pains means a triumph of mind over matter and points the way to a discipline by which the most meaningless suffering may yet be made to minister to our growth in grace. Dr. Robert Rainy, a famous Scottish church leader, once said: "There was a time in my life when my one concern

92 • COURAGE TO LIVE

was to hasten through pain and calamity at top speed. I have learned to walk through it with God and at His pace."[2]

Pain for the Christian is seen not as a hindrance to the soul to be surmounted nor as a problem to be solved but as a mystery to be lived through in faith. It is a mystery which we have to take on trust for a little while, believing that one day we shall read the mystery aright in the sunshine of God's smile. We have to learn to accept suffering as a discipline, to live with it, and to grow from it, or we will be beaten and embittered by it.

A world without suffering would be a world without much that we admire. Without hardship there would be no heroism; without pain there would be no patience; without adversity there would be no courage. Think what a rich service the sufferers render to our race! Sympathy is a shallow stream in the souls of those who have never suffered. It is true that pain does not always purify. I have known people who were hardened and embittered by the cup of suffering which they had to drink. But I have also known lives that have been transfigured by the bearing of the cross of pain. How many shallow people has pain deepened? How many hard hearts has it made tender? Suffering holds an essential place in our spiritual development. Pain is at the root of life and growth. It is not through its pleasures but through its pains that the world is carried to its highest level. Do you recall what Robert Burns wrote about pleasures?

> Pleasures are like poppies spread,
> You seize the flower, its bloom is shed![3]

Through suffering we are born, and through suffering we are fed. Through agony we have won our poetry, for we teach in song what we have learned in suffering. Through blood we have reached our freedom.

Viktor Frankl, the author of *From Death Camp to Existentialism,* is a psychiatrist who was a prisoner in a Gestapo death camp. He suffered greatly in a prison cell without adequate nourishment or proper clothing. Week after week he saw people herded to their deaths in the gas chambers. He reached the point at which life was so painful that he plotted his own suicide. Then early one morning as he lay on a bare floor, too weak to care about food, he began to look at things differently. He began believing that the kind of anguish he was witnessing and experiencing could be the prelude to a moment of great discovery. That was the turning point in his life. Later he went

THE CONQUEST OF SUFFERING • 93

about the world telling people to be receptive to their pain and open to their suffering, to stop seeing it as a grim intruder or as a mark of God's disfavor. Rather he challenged them to grow up and accept the inevitable fact that the gateway to heaven is through those who know how to mourn and to deal with sorrow.[4]

We may learn and grow through suffering, as our Lord did. He was made perfect through suffering. Life is not so much what happens to us as what happens in us. There is an Arab proverb which says, "All sunshine makes the Sahara." When Jacob wrestled with the angel, he said, "I will not let thee go, except thou bless me" (Genesis 32:26). So we may learn to say about suffering that we will not let it go until we have extracted blessing from it. Suffering may be punishment; it may be discipline, but it can also be redemptive.

The third attitude toward suffering is to look for redemption through it. Leslie Weatherhead has said that in regard to pain, whether it be physical, mental, or spiritual, we should wear bifocal glasses. The upper lens gives us distant sight and that is the lens of conquest. The lower lens gives us near sight and that is the lens of acceptance. Pain has a deep, redemptive value which we can only see when we think of it in terms of the cross. There is a very suggestive rendering, by Dr. Moffatt, of a sentence in Paul's second letter to the church in Corinth (7:10): "The pain God is allowed to guide ends in a saving repentance never to be regretted, whereas the world's pain ends in death."

I have known many sufferers who put my life to shame. From their beds of pain they have exerted far greater spiritual power than I have exerted in my active ministry. I have gone to take comfort to them and have come away having received more than I gave. Suffering when joyfully accepted carries the sufferer much further than most people go who have perfect health. The greatest sufferers I have been privileged to meet have known that suffering has been met and dealt with and is being redeemed. They have come to bless the days they spent on their back in sickness because they have learned some of the secrets of that inner life with God which we call prayer. If you will take a piece of paper and write down the names of the ten people of your acquaintance whose characters you most admire, whose lives are the kindest and the most radiant, you will discover that nearly all of them have at some time in their lives been sufferers.

It is the world's greatest sufferers who have produced the most shining examples of unconquerable faith. Pain can be creative. We do

94 • COURAGE TO LIVE

not have to bear it negatively; we can use it positively. We can compel the darkest, bitterest experiences to yield up their hidden treasures of sweetness and light. No sorrow will have been wasted if we come through it with a little more of the light of the Lord visible in our face and shining in our soul.

Our deepest need is not for explanation, to know why there is so much suffering and pain in the world, but for strength to know how it may be endured, faced, and overcome. The question "Why?" can wait. That we do not know at the moment. But the question "How?" cannot wait. We need to know how to gain the power to overcome. Helen Keller is a superb illustration of the truth of an observation she once made: "Although the world is very full of suffering, it is also full of the overcoming of it."[5] Our main concern with the dark fact of suffering is not to find an explanation but to find a victory.

Even if we were able to find a satisfying explanation of the problem of pain, that would not be enough, for the pain would still have to be borne. But the cross on Calvary transforms this age-long mystery of suffering. It tells us that God is with us in our sufferings. In every pang that rends the heart, God has a share. In every dark valley of suffering, God is present. "He healeth the broken in heart, and bindeth up their wounds" (Psalm 147:3). It is not just that God knows and sympathizes with us in our suffering. He is in us and, therefore, our suffering is his suffering; our sorrow is his sorrow.

In a fine passage in her book *Colloquia Crucis,* Dora Greenwell speaks of how, from the spectacle of life's pain and sorrow, she turned her eyes to Christ crucified. There her questions were not answered by cold and empty platitudes. She was not assured that pain was unreal, nor was she told that all was ordered for the best. Who is there who has not suffered from such cheap and worthless consolations? She says: "I was met from the eyes and brow of Him who was indeed acquainted with grief, by a look of solemn recognition, such as may pass between friends who have endured between them some strange and secret sorrow, *and are through it united in a bond that cannot be broken.*"[6]

Such is the ease that pain may find in the remembrance of Jesus. Here is One who has come to know human life in all its possibilities of pain and suffering, to know it not from the outside, "not alone as God all-knowing," but as a man. Here is One who has worn this throbbing robe of flesh, and there is not one painful throb of it that he does not feel. When pain "hunts its prey along every tortured nerve," here is a

THE CONQUEST OF SUFFERING • 95

once-suffering heart in whose wounds the hunted spirit may find sanctuary. In nights of pain and restlessness there is an inward quiet that comes with the remembrance of him who once hung "comfortless upon the cross."

In that Boston boarding house to which Oliver Wendell Holmes introduces us in his *Breakfast Table* books, one of the residents is a man, frail and deformed, whom some of his fellow boarders regard with a certain suspicion, as scarcely sound in his religious views. In that man's room there stands a locked cabinet that no one has ever seen opened. But the time comes when he dies and the cabinet is unlocked and the secret revealed. Within that closed door there hangs a crucifix, an image of the crucified Savior. In front of the cabinet the carpet is worn thin where, in many an hour of pain and loneliness, the deformed man had knelt to seek and find consolation in the sight of that other lonely Sufferer. He, too, had been met by those pain-filled eyes with that look of solemn recognition and had known that he was not bearing his burden alone. So in any suffering that may be upon us now or may wait for us in days to come, we may surely find in that same all-sufficient love divine our ease in pain.

After his wayward son has been hanged, Father Kumalo, the aged African priest in Alan Paton's novel, *Cry, the Beloved Country,* says: "I have never thought that a Christian would be free of suffering. . . . For our Lord suffered. And I came to believe that he suffered, not to save us from suffering, but to teach us how to bear suffering. For he knew that there is no life without suffering."[7] God does not sit comfortably outside our sufferings. He shares in them and that makes all the difference. If God shares in our sufferings, it is also true that we are in them with God, sharing his victory. "With his stripes we are healed" (Isaiah 53:5). Christianity is built upon a cross. Its victorious faith is founded on what looks like the worst of catastrophes, the triumphant answer to all the blackness and evil that the world contains. The cross at first glance seems like defeat, but when we look at it again, we see not Christ, the pain-racked sufferer, but Christ the mighty victor over pain. The gospel begins with the thorns in the Garden of Eden, but it ends with the One who took the thorns and wore them as a crown. He bore our griefs and carried our sorrows, but by the way he bore them and by the faith in which he carried them, he transformed the symbol of suffering into a crown of glory.

Baron Von Hugel in a letter to a friend during his last illness said: "Christ did not explain suffering. He did far more. He met it, willed it,

96 • COURAGE TO LIVE

transformed it and He taught us how to do all this or rather He Himself does it within us, if we do not hinder His all-healing hands. Suffering can be the holiest of all actions, for in suffering we are very near to God."[8] Whatever we may be called upon to suffer, it will never be anything like what our Lord suffered on the cross. If evil at its very worst has been met and mastered, as in Jesus Christ it has, if God has got his hands on this mystery of suffering and pain and turned its most awful triumph into final defeat, if that has happened, can it not happen in our lives by our union with Christ through faith?

Many things may befall Christians which will puzzle and perplex them, but nothing can happen which need finally defeat them. A scientist tells of a lady who in mistaken compassion cracked a cocoon so that the butterfly might more easily escape. She thought to save the creature a painful experience, but instead she did it an injury. For when it emerged, it was sickly and soon died. Suffering need not be a calamity. No blow can crush the soul. The same wind that blows out a match fans a flame into a fiercer glow. A severe trial will make heavy demands upon our spiritual resources, but it can be a means of spiritual enrichment. Jesus Christ can give us victory over the worst that can happen to us. If we are his, suffering may still come our way. But in his keeping we are safe and secure. This is a truth to which thousands of lives have borne witness and of which many of us have personal knowledge. This is the Christian answer to the problem of suffering: not that it may be explained, not that it may be avoided, but that it can be overcome.

12

God's Word for Eventide

**"Even to your old age I am He,
and to gray hairs I will carry you.
I have made, and I will bear;
I will carry and will save."
Isaiah 46:4, RSV**

Today the average expectation of life is higher than it ever was. When Paul wrote his letter to Philemon, he was about fifty-five; yet he called himself Paul, the aged. The average expectation of life in his day was only twenty-three. We do not reach what we consider to be old age as early as people once did. We manage to extend our lives more successfully than did our ancestors.

Few people like the idea of growing old. To some it is a cause of constant dread. Some try to disguise the fact from themselves. It is a pathetic thing when someone refuses to admit that the body is feeling the passing of the years and insists on behaving as though it were not. Such an attitude means misery for the misused body and embarrassment for others. There are many reasons for this dread of old age. The weakening of physical powers, the failure of memory, and the difficulty of taking in new ideas are often distressing. The solitude of old age is sometimes pathetic. Life is like a triangle, broad at the base

98 • COURAGE TO LIVE

but narrowing steadily as we reach the top. At the base there are many friends and kindred around us. They drop from our side one by one as we ascend the triangle. As we reach the top, we find ourselves almost alone, the old familiar faces having gone.

Ever since humans appeared on earth, they must have been seeking a gospel for old age. Some old people go on growing older gracefully. They reach a depth of maturity and conviction not possible to youth. But we do not always realize at what a cost that kind of conviction is won and kept. How easy it is for older people to slip into moods of black depression, to feel that they are no longer wanted and that the world they knew is vanishing with the passing of their friends! What is dreaded more than anything else is the seeming uselessness of old age.

Age has its penalties and its pains, but it has its glories, too. It brings a calm and serenity. At evening time it shall be light. Dr. Fosdick tells of a visitor in India who was entertained by an Indian lady of high rank. "The visitor was so impressed with her charm and grace that she could not forbear saying, 'I think you are perfectly beautiful,' to which the Indian lady quietly replied, 'I ought to be beautiful, my dear. I am seventy-four years old.'" [1] The grandeur of a great life lies in a fine finish. When we come to the eventide of our days, we find that life's flow is less noisy but how deep is the stream! The anchor of hope is not fixed on any earthly goods but on the eternal verities. The evening hours of life can bring joys and opportunities of their own. As Tennyson's brave old Ulysses says:

> Old age hath yet his honor and his toil.
> Death closes all; but something ere the end,
> Some work of noble note, may yet be done. . . .
> Tho' much is taken, much abides. . . . [2]

The evening hours are not without their tasks to which our lessening strength may still be equal. Southey speaks somewhere about "sunset pleasures." Though they lack the fierceness of the delights of the morning, they are among the best of God's gifts to his children.

Jesus spoke the same words to Simon Peter at the end of his life as at the beginning. We think of Peter setting out as a young, healthy fisherman with a bronzed face and strong muscles, in all the vigor of his manhood, and Jesus said to him, "Follow me." Then we turn the pages of the Gospel and read this: "When thou wast young, thou girdedst thyself, and walkedst whither thou wouldest: but when thou shalt be old, thou shalt stretch forth thy hands, and another shall gird thee, and carry thee whither thou wouldest not" (John 21:18). When

Christ had said this, he added, "Follow me." We remember what a dreadful death it was, how those hands, once so strong, were seized and bound, and how Peter, feeling himself unworthy to die in the same way as his Master, was crucified upside down. Yet the friendship of Jesus which transformed his youth was his comfort to the end.

To those who feel that they have passed the crest of the hill and that now their path must be slowly downward, to those who feel that they will never reach greater heights than those which lie behind them, the Master comes with his beckoning fingers and says, "Follow me." The eventide of life is in his plan. There, too, he is the same Master, Friend, and Lord.

It is good to remember what a comforting and bracing word of God there is for old age. "Even to your old age," says God, "I am he." All we have found in our best moments to be true and reliable about God and his goodness remains true, for even to old age and gray hairs he promises to carry us. The Bible is full of promises about the absolute trustworthiness of God. Whatever the experiences you have to face, passing through the waters of affliction or disappointment, they will not overwhelm you. In the furnace of pain or bereavement the flame shall not hurt you. All this is repeated and underscored on page after page of the Bible, and here it is made especially applicable to the older folk. The promises of God do not cease to apply when we pass our prime and feel that the wheels are beginning to slow down. The grace of God is ours in childhood, through the stern struggles of youth and early adulthood, through the fierce tests of middle age when we need protection against "the arrow that flieth by day," and on into old age, when we need it more than ever.

It has been truly said that "we may like better to look upon the fresh green blades of June, but it is beyond question that when the wheat is ready to be gathered, you see it at its best." What a real benediction elderly folk can be! Many achieve a ripe wisdom, a kindly sympathy, a great tolerance, and a cheery faith which makes them assets in any company and in any situation. There is nothing more beautiful than old age that has been mellowed and enriched through a long life of devotion. The biographer of the Curé of Ars says: "His heart never grew old, though the years bowed his shoulders and seamed his face. That heart seemed to know but one season—a season of endless renewal. As M. le Curé said of himself, 'In the soul united to God it is always springtime.'"[3]

100 • COURAGE TO LIVE

The psalmist says:

> They still bring forth fruit in old age,
> they are ever full of sap and green.
> (Psalm 92:14, RSV)

No one grows old merely by living many years. People grow old by denying their dreams, by deserting the high hopes which they cherished in the morning of life. Our duty is not only to add years to our lives but also to add life to our years. We need never grow old if we maintain our interest in life and in living. There is a poem of Wordsworth's addressed to his sister Dorothy which closes with these beautiful lines:

> Thy thoughts and feelings shall not die,
> Nor leave thee, when grey hairs are nigh,
> A melancholy slave;
> But an old age serene and bright,
> And lovely as a Lapland night,
> Shall lead thee to thy grave.[4]

That is the form in which Wordsworth finally left the verse. But as it was originally written, it read, "But an old age alive and bright." The earlier word, if not so musical, was very aptly chosen. Serenity in old age is beautiful to behold, but the quality suggested by the earlier word "alive" is a rarer and more enviable gift. The sad thing about some old people is not that with them old age lacks serenity, but that they are dead long before they are buried. There are others who grow lovely as they grow old.

We are as old as our fears, and as young as our faith. The answer to the question "How shall we keep young?" can be given in two words—goodness and faith. There are two sorts of age: the age of the body and the age of the mind. No one is exempt from the infirmities of age, but we need not grow old in spirit unless we give up and *be* old. The age of the body, apart from actual disease, depends on the vital organs. They get worn with wear and tear and we cannot help that. But we can keep the mind young if we face life in the right spirit, and the mind has a great influence over the body.

Some people seem quite unable to keep their minds young. They are old mentally while they are still young in years. In the full sense of the word they hardly live at all. Keep an open mind, ready to accept new ideas. You are as old as your mind, and your mind never needs to grow old. To the end of life you can go on learning. A lady from one of my former churches in England entered a Methodist Home for the

GOD'S WORD FOR EVENTIDE • 101

Aged at the age of eighty and taught herself Greek in order to be able to read the New Testament in the original. She has found endless joy in the task. Corot, the French painter, said at the age of seventy, "If God spares me for another ten years, I think I may learn to paint."[5] Unlike the flesh the spirit does not decay with the years. As Paul put it, "Though our outward man perish, yet the inward man is renewed day by day" (2 Corinthians 4:16).

Many of the happiest and most useful men and women in the world are in their sixties, seventies, and eighties. Some time ago a London doctor wrote a book entitled *How to Be Happy and Useful from Sixty to Ninety,* in which he did not hesitate to say that there is no reason why those years should not be among the best years of a person's life. But for those who have entered into this period, he emphasized the need for filling up each day as it comes with congenial, though not exacting, tasks. Again and again, he says, he has known men who led an active, strenuous life until they were sixty and then retired. Then because they had no healthy interests with which to occupy their vacant hours, they slipped swiftly down to the grave.

Some people do their finest work in old age. Gladstone, as Prime Minister of England, at eighty-three fought the greatest battle of his life for the passage of the Home Rule Bill. Goethe completed *Faust,* his greatest work, at the age of eighty-one. John Wesley wrote more than two hundred books and pamphlets and edited as many more. He averaged more than four thousand miles of travel every year, preached more than forty-two thousand sermons, and his regular practice was to travel sixty miles a day and preach at least three sermons each day. Yet, as he entered the eighty-third year of his life, he could write in his *Journal:* "I am a wonder to myself. I am never tired, either with preaching, writing or traveling." In the last year of his life, so physically spent that he had to be supported in the pulpit, he was preaching at Lowestoft and repeated, with an application of his own, these lines from "Anacreon":

> Oft am I by woman told,
> Poor Anacreon! thou growest old.
> See, thine hairs are falling all:
> Poor Anacreon! how they fall!
> Whether I grow old or no,
> By these signs, I do not know;
> But this I need not to be told
> 'Tis time to *live,* if I grow old.[6]

102 • COURAGE TO LIVE

John Wesley grew old gracefully, like the old man of whom Dr. J. H. Jowett used to speak, a man whose face reminded him of a ruined chapel away in the country, with all the lamps inside lighted up for the evening service. Goodness, or, as the Bible likes to call it, righteousness, is the first element of character that arrests decay and makes even old age bear fruit.

The second element of character which keeps the heart young is faith. Faith implies a hold upon the spiritual. It is faith in someone or something that makes life worth living. A great faith keeps one young. Think of the aged Simeon holding in his arms the infant Jesus in the temple. He had the lovely face which God gives to those who love him. Though his life on earth was nearly over, Simeon was still interested in the future. Life had not soured him nor taken away his hope. He fulfilled the words of the prophet Joel, "Your old men shall dream dreams." Dr. Jung, the famous Swiss psychologist, said that many people "approach the threshold of old age with unsatisfied claims which inevitably turn their glances backwards." They live in the past. They have memories but no dreams, and they are petulant and bitter. Simeon was not like that. There was a light of hope on his brow and a fire of dreams in his eyes. He was looking for the Lord, waiting for the consolation of Israel.

The same faith that possessed Simeon must have been in the Quaker who, at the age of eighty-two, said, "I'm going to live till I die and then I'm going to live forever." Victor Hugo said of himself, "The snows of winter are on my head but eternal spring is in my heart." [7] He declared that, though he had written much, he had not written a thousandth part of what was in him, and therefore he had absolute faith in a future life. There is a famous saying of the Greek poet Theocritus, "Those whom the gods love die young." That does not mean that the fortunate people are cut off by death in their early days but that the persons whom the gods have blessed feel young at whatever age they die. Eternal spring is in their hearts.

If we hold on to this great promise of God that even to our old age he will still be the same, that when we are gray-haired, he will still sustain us, then we shall be able to keep our faith sweet and strong, always growing and making fresh discoveries of God to the end of our days. God is our guide even unto death and beyond death, as Jesus has told us, into the better country, which is our homeland.

May Robson, an American film actress who so often portrayed an old lady, once wrote these lines:

GOD'S WORD FOR EVENTIDE • 103

Age is a quality of mind.
If you have left your dreams behind,
If hope is cold,
If you no longer look ahead,
If your ambition's fires are dead,
Then you are old.

But if from life you take the best,
And if in life you see the jest,
If to love, you hold,
Then, no matter how the years go by,
No matter how the birthdays fly,
You are not old.[8]

She lived up to this affirmation of her faith. She said, "When your name is called, and you join the fold, the thing that counts is what you have left behind—not riches, jewels, or fame—but the legacy of love which death defies."

In the Old Testament, people dreaded old age because it brought death near, and death, if not the end, was a melancholy experience. They were always pleading with God for length of days. Length of life was the great reward of almost everything, even honoring your father and mother. "With long life will I satisfy him, and shew him my salvation" (Psalm 91:16). "What man is he that desireth life, and loveth many days, that he may see good?" (Psalm 34:12). The sad thing was that, as for man, his days were as grass.

The New Testament altered all that. Jesus was certain of the life beyond, so much so that Paul could not make up his mind whether he would rather die or live. He said, "I am in a strait betwixt two, having a desire to depart, and to be with Christ; which is far better" (Philippians 1:23). In his last days he wrote to Timothy, "I am now ready to be offered. . . . I have fought a good fight, I have finished my course, I have kept the faith: Henceforth there is laid up for me a crown of righteousness" (2 Timothy 4:6-8). Here was a man at the end of life, strangely content. He had no regrets, though none of the prizes of life had come his way. He had found a leader and a cause to which he gave his all. He was a man subtly changed, mellow, kindly, tolerant, patient, so different from what he had been as a persecutor of the Christians. Paul was a man full of faith and hope, still as sure of God and his love as ever he had been. He had kept the faith though he had a great deal to endure which might have caused him to lose it.

When we were born, there were hands to welcome us into this

104 • COURAGE TO LIVE

world, eyes that smiled into ours, arms that held us closely, and loving people who wanted us. Will God who provided for our entry into this life on earth forget us when we leave it? Will there not be hands to draw us in and eyes that smile at us in welcome? Will there not be blessed reunions and the spirit of joyous adventure in the world beyond death? If old age is in some sense a second childhood, it is because those soon to be with God are given a final opportunity to become as little children.

There is a lovely story told of Saint Columba. He was old. His work was done and he was eager to start out on the last journey. A brother came to his cell, looked at him for a while, and then said roughly, "You are dying," at which a wonderful light blazed into the dying man's eyes. Then Columba, looking up, smiled and said, "I am not dying. My body, yes, but I—I cannot die. My spirit is his home and my Dear One is within the house." There was a man who had proved the truth of the promise of God, "Even to your old age I am He, and to gray hairs I will carry you."

13

How to Grieve with Hope

"We would not have you ignorant, brethren, concerning those who are asleep, that you may not grieve as others do who have no hope." 1 Thessalonians 4:13 (RSV)

Grief is as old as humanity. Four thousand years ago on a sunny day in Egypt, heartbroken parents laid to rest in a carved sarcophagus the body of their little daughter. A few years ago two English explorers discovered the tomb in a cave which had been shut up all that time and on the tomb were inscribed the words, "O my life, my love, my little one. Would God I had died for thee."[1] The two explorers returned from the darkness of the cave with dim eyes into the blazing sunshine of the Egyptian desert. Then they sealed the entrance, leaving love and death to their eternal vigil.

Grief is a universal emotion. None of us is able to escape it. From the beginning God created us to live for a while on earth and then to die. Death is an inevitable ingredient of life. With death comes grief. We grieve not so much over what has happened to our loved ones as over what has happened to us. We are left more alone. Grief comes because of separation from the one we care about. But the experience

106 • COURAGE TO LIVE

of grief is not limited to the death of a loved one. We grieve over the loss of some thing or some person important to us Someone who has a leg or an arm amputated suffers grief. When a romance is broken up, young people feel grief. A child grieves when the ragged, little, stuffed animal is thrown away because parents think it is too old and dirty to keep. When someone or something that has become part of a person's pattern of emotional satisfaction and security is removed, grief ensues.

We all experience grief. Our problem is how to face the days ahead of us without being overwhelmed by our grief. In our grief we feel that nothing remains for us but a lonely journey through the years. Often we are able to manage the initial shock of loss with what one writer has called "cornered courage." We rise to the occasion and carry on supported by our friends and neighbors. We shed tears without shame, and everyone understands. But then comes the loneliness and the inability to think of anything but our loss. We sometimes experience feelings of guilt. We wish that we had been more thoughtful and considerate. Grief is multiplied by regret.

The victory over grief is one of the most important and critical of all victories, for so many people are conquered by their grief. How many such people I have seen in my ministry! On the other hand, I have seen a great many who were able to sing songs in the night and who came off more than conquerors through him who loved them. Sorrow is a cup which all must drink. As an old Spanish proverb says: "There is no home on earth but will have its hush." The prophet speaks of the treasures of darkness. (See Isaiah 45:3). In the darkness of grief we must look for hidden treasure and believe that God makes no mistakes. I told a young woman who had lost her husband, whom she loved dearly, that after the first paroxysm of grief was over, calmness would come to her spirit and she would see how God could bring good out of this affliction. She answered, "No. Nothing good can come out of it." If you take that attitude toward God, nothing good will come out of it for you; but if you trust even when you cannot see, good will come.

Jesus said, "Blessed are those who mourn, for they shall be comforted" (Matthew 5:4). To be comforted in the face of loss, we must work through our grief and handle our sorrow. There is no easy grief. There are no easy ways to work through grief quickly and painlessly. But grief may become good grief if we react to it aright. Thomas Erskine of Linlathen in one of his letters wrote:

HOW TO GRIEVE WITH HOPE • 107

> A lost sorrow is so sad a thing. A sorrow in which God has spoken to His creature, and called it to feel that there is no Helper but Himself, and that He is there present to comfort, and sustain, and bless,—such a sorrow to be neglected and thrown off by the creature, and forgotten as soon as possible, is it not wonderful, and as sad as wonderful?[2]

Life is meant to be richer and deeper through the experience of sorrow. The great thing is not to "get over" a sorrow but rather to get right into it and to find at the very heart of it the presence of God. For God is always there, and never quite so near as in the time of grief.

The story of the raising of Lazarus as told in John's Gospel is most helpful in understanding something of the nature of grief. The opening verses clearly show the depth of the friendship shared by Jesus and the family of Lazarus. "It was Mary who anointed the Lord with ointment and wiped his feet with her hair. . . ." The message sent to Jesus by the sisters of Lazarus said simply, "Lord, he whom you love is ill" (John 11:2, 3, RSV). They sensed no need to ask Jesus to come, for they knew that he would. He had spent many happy hours in that home in Bethany. Even in the face of extreme danger and against the advice of his disciples, Jesus went to be with Mary and Martha in their time of need.

Grief is a time of such bitter loneliness that we need our friends with us. John tells us that many Jews had come to be with Mary and Martha. It was a sacred duty to express loving sympathy. Jesus knew, as we know, that the grief-stricken sufferer needs support from others. The presence of friends can help to fill the terrible void that is felt. However, to encourage the person to be brave and to realize that the loved one is "better off now" only increases the isolation caused by grief. A feeling of numbness usually engulfs the sufferer soon after the death. What we say is seldom remembered. Our presence is what is important, for the person realizes that we care and want to offer our support. When the grieved want to talk about the one they have lost, we ought to encourage this. For the more death is talked about, the sooner the reality of what has happened is accepted.

Grief is an emotion which can be forced out of consciousness and be denied or delayed, but it can never be destroyed. It must be faced and worked through. Elizabeth Gray Vining in her autobiography, *Quiet Pilgrimage,* describes the death of her husband in a car crash and says: "Gradually I learned . . . that grief is something not to overcome or to escape but to live with. It is always there . . . but one can make room for it, recognize it as a companion instead of an

108 • COURAGE TO LIVE

intruder, be aware of it but not possessed by it; one can continue one's work, one's occupations, even one's joys in its presence."[3]

When Mary left the house to go and meet Jesus, the Jews thought that she was going to the tomb to weep. This seemed natural to them. Sorrow must be expressed. Under the stress of grief, weeping is not a sign of weakness. On the contrary, honest tears are nothing to be ashamed of. We say, "Big boys don't cry." Why not? We say, "If she had enough faith, she would hold up." Faith has nothing to do with it. We can truly believe that our loved one is with God, that God is with us to comfort and support us, and that things will work out, but we still hurt because of the separation. There is a Hebrew proverb about "wearing out grief"—"If you bottle it up, you will never soften it." Shakespeare in *Macbeth* says:

> Give sorrow words: the grief that does not speak
> Whispers the o'er-fraught heart, and bids it break.[4]

Edmund Spenser in *The Faerie Queen* says: "He oft finds present help who does his grief impart."[5] The person who holds himself tense and refuses to let go may be in for trouble. Jesus wept at the grave of Lazarus. He was "a man of sorrows and acquainted with grief." We must face and admit honestly "the tears in things." Grief must work itself out. God cannot wipe away our tears until we have faced our grief.

Grief must be accepted, not in a grim, bitter, fatalistic way but as a fact of life. Jeremiah said: "Woe is me for my hurt! my wound is grievous: but I said, Truly this is a grief, and I must bear it" (Jeremiah 10:19). We must try to accept our grief as our share of the sorrow of the world, a sorrow which God himself eternally shares. All experience is a school in which God sets us to learn. But it would seem that suffering is one of the higher forms in God's school and one through which almost all those must pass whom God would teach the deepest secret of his love or train for worthiest service. Even Jesus had to learn that part of God's school. "It became [God] . . . in bringing many sons unto glory, to make the captain of their salvation perfect through sufferings" (Hebrews 2:10). If God's beloved Son needed that discipline, shall any of his children expect otherwise to master life's deepest lessons or to gain life's greatest gifts?

We find it all too easy to cherish bitter thoughts when those who are dearest to us slip from our grasp. But in bitterness there is no healing and no help. The best way of reacting to grief is to sit down

HOW TO GRIEVE WITH HOPE • 109

and confront it. Do not try to put it out of your mind. Put it in the center of your mind and say, "This is my grief and I must bear it." But then go on to say, "How can I turn this into an asset? How can I make this grief of mine serve God's purpose in my life?" It can be made to serve him. It will make us more sympathetic with others. In some hour when another calls upon us, it will strengthen our advice. It may even break our pride. Whatever happens to us can be woven into the purpose of God. Even the cross was willed by wicked men, but God wove it into the redemption of the world. And our thorns, like Christ's, can become a crown.

It is always at the time of grief that the gospel moves in. Was not this when God came that day in the Garden of Eden to Adam and Eve, who had lost something? That was why strange things happened in Egypt to a group of slaves who had lost their freedom. We follow their trail across the desert to the Promised Land and later into exile from that land. We read the story of Job, who was covered with boils and whose heart was well-nigh broken. We see Jeremiah weep for his country that was lost. Then Isaiah picks up the theme in his Servant Song, dreaming of One who will bear our griefs and carry our sorrows. Luke carries on the tradition as he speaks of what Jesus is to do. "He came to heal the brokenhearted." The members of the early church, as they looked over their shoulders at so much grief and looked around them at persecution and losses, sum it all up for us. "We would not have you ignorant, brethren, concerning those who are asleep, that you may not grieve as others do who have no hope" (1 Thessalonians 4:13, RSV).

In the Christian gospel there is not an absence of grief but something greater. We find grief made bearable; we discover grief made livable. We must come to terms with grief transformed. It is a grief that heals and strengthens, a good grief. The New Testament promises comfort to the grief-stricken. The word "comfort" comes from two Latin words, *con* and *fortis*. It means literally "strengthened by being with." It is a reinforcing of the heart with strength and courage. There is a light for our darkness and strength for our weakness. The blessing pronounced on the mourners is a blessing which belongs only to God's people and to them here and now. It is not pronounced over those who make a luxury of grief. There are people who are never so happy as when they are miserable. There can be no blessing for them, for such mourning is self-indulgence. True mourning finds us neither pitying ourselves nor wringing our hands

110 • COURAGE TO LIVE

in despair. It lays bare our inadequacy and drives us back upon God. Without a belief in God, sorrow would be an unrelieved tragedy, as hard to explain as to escape.

The path of the aching heart leads to the comfort of God's peace. We learn that we are not alone. God is in the midst of our grief, not to explain it, but to share it. He shall wipe away our tears, for he comes to us from the heart of a cross, understanding the agony of grief. We do not grieve as those do who have no hope. Martha's faith is seen in what she says to Jesus. "I know that whatever you ask of God, God will give you. . . . I know that he [Lazarus] will rise again in the resurrection at the last day" (John 11:22, 24, RSV). She believed in the resurrection of the dead. She was sure that life did not end here and that humanity was not alone in this world. After death is resurrection. Physical death does not end it all.

Jesus revealed to this grieving family the fullness of God's love and care. "Jesus . . . was deeply moved in spirit and troubled" (John 11:33, RSV). He came to reveal to us the truth that God is One who feels our hurt, who suffers with us, and knows our pain. He showed us a God whose very heart is wrung with anguish in the anguish of his people, a God who in the most literal way is afflicted in our afflictions.

Our faith will not help us to escape grief; it will not remove the necessity of working through grief. It will not cover our grief, but it can assist us in facing grief and in knowing that we do not face it alone. Faith can help us to pick up the broken pieces of life and to begin a life lived for others. This is what happened to Catherine Marshall in the two experiences of grief which came to her. First, she contracted tuberculosis. This required complete bed rest for her and a major change in the life of her family. For months nothing happened. She was no better and sometimes worse. But one day, at the very depths of her grief over the loss of health, she reached out for the very first time for God and found him. She tells about her growing experience in her book, *A Man Called Peter*. Later, when Peter Marshall died and she was devastated by the loss of her husband, there came a second touch. God came and led her through her grief. For the first time she tried to set down on paper what she felt. Today Catherine Marshall's name is known everywhere because, in her grief, she learned to write and thereby she has helped millions of people.

When our grief is faced and accepted, the resources of the spirit bring strength to transform it. In the historic King's Chapel in Boston, Massachussetts, there is a box-pew on which is a plaque with these words engraved on it: "Theodore Pickering, Litt.D. One who could share in the whole world's tears, And still be glad." [6] He was born during the dark days of the Civil War and died during World War I. "He must have been a sensitive man to be described as sharing the whole world's tears." [7] This is what God does. As we walk through the valley of the shadow of death, he is with us; his rod and staff comfort us. So we need not fear the dark clouds with which life overshadows us, because we know that we shall always find God in them, the God who wipes the tears from every eye, the God through whose loving wisdom no grief is without its gain.

14

Looking Death in the Face[1]

"It is appointed unto men once to die. . . ." Hebrews 9:27
"Christ . . . hath abolished death. . . ." 2 Timothy 1:10

Death stands at the end of our existence like a great, gray question mark. It throws a long shadow back over our days, and we live in this shadow. We try to dispel it by living hard or pretending that it is not there. But death remains the final enigma, the unresolved question, the haunting mystery. It comes under many guises. At the end of a long fruitful life it comes with quiet and easy naturalness. After long suffering it comes as a welcome release. But often it comes shockingly, even crudely—the sharp crack of an assassin's rifle, the crash of a car or a plane, a sudden heart seizure, or the erosion of cancer.

Let us look death full in the face without flinching, without evasion, without terror. From the time written of Adam and Eve in the Garden of Eden, "Thou shalt surely die," to Paul's vivid assertion that death is the final enemy to be conquered, and down to the latest funeral, we have shrunk from looking squarely at death. We evade it.

113

114 • COURAGE TO LIVE

We will not talk about it. We will not even say of a person that "he died" but instead we say "he passed away." We skirt it delicately with our loved ones in their last illness, and at funerals we powder and paint it out of all semblance of reality. We hope that medical science, which has lengthened our life by some years, will soon have done away with death completely, but it will not. The irony of it all is that while we have this feeling that death should not be mentioned, death is all around us. We read of it in the newspapers and see it on television—violence in the streets, traffic accidents, death in war. We are surrounded by death, and yet we seem incapable of saying the word.

Death is one of the very few things that can be safely predicted of all of us. There are not many things you can say with absolute certainty of everyone, but this is one: "It is appointed unto men once to die..." (Hebrews 9:27). We all have a rendezvous with death. What folly, therefore, it is to avoid facing the fact and what a stupid convention it is which would hide this solemn event from us or lead us to ignore its challenge! "We know that we are going to die," says Dr. Alex Munthe in his book *The Story of San Michele,* "in fact it is the only thing we know of what is in store for us. All the rest is mere guesswork, and most of the time we guess wrong."[2]

In the Hollywood Cemetery in Richmond, Virginia, there is a quaint epitaph:

> Pause, stranger, as you pass by,
> As you are now, so once was I,
> As I am now so you must be,
> Therefore prepare to follow me.

That verse constitutes a kindly warning and a worthy suggestion. Every man must be prepared for the great adventure of death. Death is no respecter of persons. It comes to all ages and invades all situations. Sometimes it comes without warning, but more often it comes with adequate notice and suffcent time for us to prepare to meet it.

Death is "the shadow fear'd of man." I once heard Dr. Sangster say: "A man is either very sick of earth or very sure of heaven who does not shrink from death." The fear of death is as old as human life, as long as human life, and as widespread as human life. Some fear it more than others, but we all fear it more at certain periods of life than at others. In youth we hardly give it a thought. But when the middle years come and old friends begin to leave us, how can we help but say

LOOKING DEATH IN THE FACE • 115

to ourselves, "It will not always be someone else's funeral; some day it will be mine"? Jesus came, says the writer of the Epistle to the Hebrews, that he might "deliver them who through fear of death were all their lifetime subject to bondage" (Hebrews 2:15).

Dr. Samuel Johnson had an overmastering fear of the end. "Oh, my friend," he wrote as he saw it coming near," the approach of death is very terrible. I am afraid to think on that which I know I cannot avoid. It is vain to look round for that help which cannot be had."[3] Why is there such a fear of death? For one thing, we have an understandable fear of the unknown, the mystery of a change of which we have no experience, the hurt of leaving things that we find so pleasant here. O. Henry, the famous American writer, said to his nurse as his feet were going down into the valley of the shadow, "Bring me a candle." When she asked him why he wanted a candle, he replied, "Because I am afraid to go home in the dark."[4]

Another reason for our fear of death is that we dread the separation from loved ones and the loneliness which it brings. There is also the fear of death's pain, the fear that death may be attended by circumstances of special trouble or distress. Doctors assure us that what is normally called "the agony of death" is felt much more by the bedside watchers than by the one who is dying. Sir William Osler, a noted physician, said that very few people actually experience fear at the time of death. Of five hundred deaths he studied with this question in mind, only eleven showed apprehension, and only two any signs of terror. Dr. Alfred Worcester, a former professor of hygiene at Harvard, said: "Death is almost always preceded by a perfect willingness to die. I have never seen it otherwise. It is always easy at the last. However great the previous suffering, there is always an interval of peace, and often of ecstasy, before death."[5]

Some of us, when we think of death and what lies beyond it, create needless difficulties for ourselves. We try to imagine a life in which all the familiar conditions of our earthly lives have no part. We tease ourselves with questions to which we have no answer. Our faculties are unable to conceive the nature of the life to come. Our ignorance is no argument against its reality. The unborn babe in its mother's womb has no conception of the life upon which it is soon to enter. Yet that life is there, real, warm, and friendly, and presently the little one finds its home within it. In like fashion may we not say that though eye has not seen, nor ear heard, nor has it entered into the heart to imagine the things which God has prepared for those who love him,

116 • COURAGE TO LIVE

they are not less really there, though our knowledge is so small and the eye of faith is so dim?

We are not free in life unless we are free from the fear of death. We certainly cannot be rid of it by not thinking about it; but, on the contrary, only by becoming accustomed to it, by learning to be at home in it do we snatch from it its greatest advantage over us, its strangeness. When we do face death bravely and honestly, what happens? Its terrors vanish. That is true of all fears. To face our fears is to tame them. To be willing to look death full in the face is already to be above death.

How can we learn to look death full in the face and with courage? Through faith in Christ. It is he who makes us more than conquerors over death, for he "hath abolished death, and hath brought life and immortality to light through the gospel" (2 Timothy 1:10). With Christ we can stare death in the face and be unafraid. For he died, but in death he conquered death. In him therefore death loses all its terror. So, as Paul says: ". . . Death is swallowed up in victory. O death, where is thy sting? O grave, where is thy victory? . . . Thanks be to God, which giveth us the victory through our Lord Jesus Christ" (1 Corinthians 15:54-57).

John Donne, the poet-preacher of the early seventeenth century, wrote this magnificent defiance of death:

> Death be not proud, though some have called thee
> Mighty and dreadful, for thou art not so;
> For those whom thou think'st thou dost overthrow
> Die not, poor Death, nor yet canst thou kill me.
>
> One short sleep past, we wake eternally,
> And death shall be no more, death, thou shalt die.[6]

The life, death, and resurrection of Jesus Christ, his presence and his power, take away the fear of death, the foreboding of judgment and the uncertainty of immortality. Christ has, as it were, even redeemed immortality, for that means much more than just life continuing. It means a new quality of life like his own. We do not go on being what we are. We become like him, for we shall see him as he is. Hence we can face death with serenity, knowing that as "it is appointed unto men once to die," in Christ, death means new life. Christ has abolished death. Can we believe that? Look at the Greek word translated "abolished." It means "to make barren," "to take the heart out of," "to put down," "to conquer," "to devitalize." That is the

LOOKING DEATH IN THE FACE • 117

bold claim Paul makes. Christ has devitalized death. He has taken the life out of it. He has made it of no effect. How has the Prince of Life done this?

First, by his teaching. Read your New Testament with a view to noticing how our Lord used the word "death." Only once does he use it where we would have used it. Normally where we would use the word "death," he uses the word "sleep." He used it with such consistency and discrimination as to exclude the fact that it was for him a figure of speech. To the mourners standing around the breathless body of the daughter of Jairus, he said, "She is not dead, but sleepeth" (Luke 8:52). To the disciples concerning Lazarus already laid in the tomb, he remarked, "Our friend Lazarus sleepeth; but I go, that I may awake him out of sleep." They were so slow to understand their Master's mind that they said, "Lord, if he sleep, he shall do well." Then, as a concession to their dullness of mind, he used the word "death" as they would use it. "Then said Jesus unto them plainly, Lazarus is dead" (John 11:11–14). Where we would use the word "death," he used the word "sleep." He took the dread out of the thing by changing the word. He devitalized death in his teaching by refusing to regard the end of our physical activities as something final. Florence Allshorn near the end of her life wrote to a friend:

I can never see why one should fear to die. When I walk into the garden here early in the morning and nearly burst with excitement at this world and when I realize that it is only a shadow, a pale ghost of what that world must be like, then I can only feel a tremendous longing to know more of it and to be in it.[7]

Christ also devitalized death by his cross. The great cause of human misery is sin. The vital principle of death is sin. Most of Paul's letters bear witness to that, and we do not understand the gospel at all if we do not know that the cross and sin were somehow for our redemption most wonderfully related. Paul says so plainly. "Christ died for our sins" (1 Corinthians 15:3), and he died that we need not die. We cannot save ourselves from our sins, from the guilt of past sin, nor yet from the consequences of sin in death. Only Christ can do that. He devitalized death because he dealt with sin in his cross.

But Christ most completely devitalized death by his rising again. The cross would have been all darkness had not the light from the empty tomb streamed back upon it and lit up that darkest hour in human history to make it the brightest hour of all. Shakespeare called death "that undiscovered country from whose bourne no traveller

118 • COURAGE TO LIVE

returns." He was wrong. One traveler came back. Christ went stalking through death like somebody blazing a trail through undiscovered country, carrying the frontiers with him, heading straight for the lands beyond the sunset and bringing back with him the title deeds.

The conquest of death is the final achievement of religion. Christianity came into the world as a death-conquering religion. It centered in the figure of One who had conquered death and made it of no account. As a final darkness it was no longer there. Dawn had broken over the hills. Christ had abolished death not as a fact but as a terror. Death stands in our lives as a perpetual reminder that this life is not all, that our little lives go out into mystery. One evening, toward the close of General Booth's life, his daughter found him in his study, very weak and almost completely blind. The window looked out over the countryside, and there was a lovely sunset. "Can you see it?" she asked her father. "No, I cannot see it," he said. She led him nearer to the window and helped him up, but it was no use. "No, my dear," he said, "I cannot see the sunset but I shall see the sunrise."[8] That is what death means for the Christian, the sunrise over the Father's house.

On April 8, 1945, Dietrich Bonhoeffer held a service in the Flossenburg prison. He had hardly finished his last prayer when the door opened and two men came in and said, "Prisoner Bonhoeffer, get ready to come with us." He said to an English officer who was a fellow prisoner, "This is the end. . . . For me the beginning of life."[9] The next day he was hanged. For every Christian, whether the summons comes soon or late, this should be the meaning of death— the beginning of life in another dimension of existence. Death releases us from the limitations of the body and the weakness of the flesh and introduces us to a larger, fuller life, with greater opportunities of growth and service.

The Dean and Chaplain of Westminster Abbey offered a place in death for the founder of the Boy Scout movement, Lord Baden-Powell, between the grave of the unknown soldier and that of David Livingstone. But after careful consideration the family decided to decline the offer, and they buried him in a grave in Kenya with full military honors and a guard of Boy Scouts from Europe, Asia, and Africa. On the simple stone which they erected is carved a circle with a dot in the center of it, which is the Scout trail sign meaning, "I have gone home." That is what death means to the Christian—going home to the Father's house.

LOOKING DEATH IN THE FACE • 119

A Christian missionary captured by Communists and facing certain death wrote a letter to a friend which included a poem in which she expressed her thoughts about her anticipated martyrdom.

> Afraid of death? Afraid? Of what?
> Afraid to see the Savior's face?
> To hear His welcome and to trace
> The glory gleam from wounds of grace?
> Afraid? Of that? [10]

Everything is different now that Christ has fought and beaten death. It has no terrors for us now, for we know that we pass from death unto life, from darkness to light.

At the southernmost point of South Africa is a cape around which the storms are always raging. For a thousand years no one knew what lay beyond that cape, for no ship had ever returned to tell the tale. It was called the Cape of Storms. In the sixteenth century a Portuguese explorer, Vasco da Gama, successfully sailed around the cape and found beyond it a great calm sea and beyond that the shores of India. So the name of the cape was changed to the Cape of Good Hope. Till Christ rose from the dead, death had been the Cape of Storms on which the hopes of all mankind were wrecked, and no one knew what lay beyond it. But now that Christ has risen from the dead, it has become for all who believe in him the Cape of Good Hope, and we know that beyond it lie the shores of heaven.

Notes

CHAPTER 1

[1] Lloyd Douglas, *Green Light* (Boston: Houghton Mifflin Company, 1935).

[2] Adam W. Fergusson, *Bruce of Banff* (Edinburgh: Andrew Elliott, 1934), p. 209.

[3] W. Mackintosh Mackay, *Problems in Living* (London: Hodder and Stoughton Ltd., 1935), p. 19.

CHAPTER 2

[1] Paul S. Rees, *The Adequate Man* (Old Tappan: Fleming H. Revell Company, 1959), p. 111.

[2] Leonard Griffith, *This Is Living* (Nashville: Abingdon Press, 1966), p. 134.

[3] Joseph Medlicott Scriven, "What a Friend We Have in Jesus."

[4] George Matheson, *Day unto Day* (Old Tappan: Fleming H. Revell Company, 1908), p. 144.

[5] W. E. Sangster, *Why Jesus Never Wrote a Book* (London: Epworth Press, 1932), pp. 41-42.

122 • COURAGE TO LIVE

CHAPTER 3

[1] Jill Morgan, *Campbell Morgan; a Man of the Word* (Old Tappan: Fleming H. Revell Company, 1951), p. 60.

[2] *Life and Letters of Mandell Creighton* by his wife (London: Longmans, Green, & Co., Ltd., 1904), vol. 1, p. 245.

[3] Constance Padwick, *Henry Martyn* (London: Church Missionary Society, 1925), pp. 190-191.

[4] Quoted in J. S. Stewart, *The Wind of the Spirit* (London: Hodder and Stoughton, Ltd., 1968), p. 20.

CHAPTER 4

[1] Quoted in George Jackson, *A Parson's Log* (London: Epworth Press, 1927), p. 176.

[2] Morris L. West, *The Shoes of the Fisherman* (New York: William Morrow & Co., Inc., 1963), p. 92.

[3] Letter written on September 5, 1893, in *Selected Letters of R. L. Stevenson* (London: Methuen & Co. Ltd., 1920), pp. 267-268.

[4] John Milton, "22nd Sonnet to Cyriack Skinner" in *The Complete Poetical Works of John Milton* (Boston: Houghton Mifflin Company, 1924), p. 78.

[5] James Watt quoted in Harry Emerson Fosdick, *The Meaning of Faith* (New York: Association Press, 1942), p. 133.

[6] Helen Keller quoted in Charles L. Allen, *Healing Words* (Old Tappan: Fleming H. Revell Company, 1961), p. 85.

[7] Ralph Waldo Emerson, "The Fable" in *Poems* (Boston: Houghton Mifflin Company, 1904), p. 75.

[8] Harry Emerson Fosdick, *The Power to See It Through* (New York: Harper & Row, Publishers, 1935), p. 51.

[9] Quoted in Jackson, *op. cit.,* p. 188.

CHAPTER 5

[1] Harry Emerson Fosdick, *On Being a Real Person* (New York: Harper & Row, Publishers, 1943), p. 188.

[2] William Wordsworth, "The Prelude," Book XI, *The Complete Poetical Works of Wordsworth* (Boston: Houghton Mifflin Company, 1932), p. 205.

[3] Percy Ainsworth, *The Pilgrim Church and Other Sermons* (Old Tappan: Fleming H. Revell Company, n.d.), p. 185.

NOTES • 123

[4] *Selected Poems of F. W. H. Myers* (London: Macmillan & Co. Ltd., 1870), p. 12.

[5] Quoted in F. B. James, *For the Quiet Hour* (London: Epworth Press, 1937), p. 117.

[6] Quoted in *ibid.*.

[7] Quoted in Robert J. McCracken, *Questions People Ask* (New York: Harper & Row, Publishers, 1951), p. 143.

[8] Quoted in W. Mackintosh Mackay, *Problems in Living* (London: Hodder and Stoughton, Ltd., 1935), p. 200.

[9] Fosdick, *op. cit.*, p. 194.

CHAPTER 6

[1] R. J. McCracken, *Questions People Ask* (New York: Harper & Row, Publishers, 1951), p. 125.

[2] W. E. Sangster, *The Secret of Radiant Life* (Nashville: Abingdon Press, 1957), p. 82.

[3] Harry Emerson Fosdick, *The Hope of the World* (New York: Harper & Row, Publishers, 1953), p. 124.

[4] Charles E. Macartney, *You Can Conquer* (Nashville: Abingdon Press, 1954), p. 18.

[5] Charles Wesley, Hymn No. 355, verse 8, in *A Collection of Hymns for the use of the People Called Methodists* (London: 1780).

CHAPTER 7

[1] *Collected Poems of Rupert Brooke* (London: Sidgwick & Jackson, Ltd. n.d.), p. lxxxi.

[2] Tennyson quoted in W. E. Sangster, *Westminster Sermons,* vol. 2 (London: Epworth Press, 1961), p. 48.

[3] Alan Moorehead, *Eclipse* (New York: Harper & Row, Publishers, 1945), p. 98.

[4] Stopford Brooke, *Life and Letters of F. W. Robertson,* vol. 1 (London: Henry S. King, 1866), pp. 187-188.

CHAPTER 8

[1] Rudyard Kipling, "If" in *Rudyard Kipling's Verse* (New York: Doubleday, Doran, and Company, Inc., 1938), p. 648.

[2] Charles Wesley, Hymn No. 874, verse 7, *Methodist Hymn Book* (London: Epworth Press, 1933).

124 • COURAGE TO LIVE

[3] Leslie D. Weatherhead, *How Can I Find God?* (London: Hodder and Stoughton Ltd., 1933), p. 256.

[4] Quoted in Harry Emerson Fosdick, *Twelve Tests of Character* (New York: Association Press, 1923), p. 60.

CHAPTER 9

[1] Harry Emerson Fosdick, *The Meaning of Prayer* (New York: Association Press, 1951), p. 17.

[2] William Shakespeare, *Hamlet,* in *The Works of William Shakespeare* (New York: Oxford University Press, Inc., 1938), act 3, sc. 3, lines 39-40.

[3] Longfellow quoted in Fosdick, *op. cit.,* p. 111.

[4] Quoted in Fosdick, *op. cit.,* p. 120.

[5] Hugh Crichton-Miller, *The New Psychology and the Preacher* (London: Jarrolds Publishers, 1926), p. 209.

[6] Margaret Blair Johnstone, *When God Says No* (New York: Simon & Schuster, Inc., 1954), p. 8.

[7] Quoted in Fosdick, *op. cit.,* p. 124.

[8] Dom Bernard Clements, *When Ye Pray* (London: S.C.M. Press Ltd., 1936), pp. 91-92.

[9] Hymn No. 433, verse 2, trans. John Wesley, *Methodist Hymn Book* (London: Epworth Press, 1933).

[10] Quoted from Fosdick, *op. cit.,* p. 70.

[11] Charles Wesley, Hymn No. 465, verse 2, *Methodist Hymn Book.*

[12] John Oxenham, *A Saint in the Making* (London: Longmans, Green & Co. Ltd., 1931), p. 82.

CHAPTER 10

[1] From a sermon by Leslie D. Weatherhead in *The City Temple Tidings* for September, 1959.

[2] W. R. Maltby, *The Meaning of the Cross* (London: Epworth Press, 1926), p. 10.

[3] "Jesus, United by Thy Grace," Hymn No. 193, verse 2, *Methodist Hymnal* (Nashville: The Methodist Publishing House, 1966).

[4] William Blake, *Selected Poetry and Prose of William Blake,* ed. Northrop Frye (New York: Random House, Inc., 1953), p. 34.

NOTES • 125

[5] Marc Connelly, *The Green Pastures* (New York: Holt, Rinehart and Winston, Inc., 1929), pp. 172-173. Copyright 1929, 1930, © 1957, 1958 by Marc Connelly. Reprinted with permission of Holt, Rinehart and Winston, Publishers.

[6] Dr. and Mrs. Howard Taylor, *Hudson Taylor and the China Inland Mission* (London: Religious Tract Society, 1927), p. 291.

[7] Bishop William Quayle, quoted in Harry Emerson Fosdick, *On Being a Real Person* (New York: Harper & Row, Publishers, p. 143), p. 250.

CHAPTER 11

[1] C. S. Lewis, *The Problem of Pain* (New York: The Macmillan Company, 1945), p. 81.

[2] Carnegie Simpson, *Life of Principal Rainy* (London: Hodder and Stoughton Ltd., 1909), vol. 2, p. 468.

[3] Robert Burns, "Tam O' Shanter" in *The Poetical Works of Robert Burns* (Philadelphia: J. B. Lippincott and Co., 1881), p. 132.

[4] Viktor Frankl, *From Death Camp to Existentialism* (Boston: Beacon Press, 1959).

[5] Helen Keller quoted by Lowell R. Ditzen, *Personal Security Through Faith* (New York: Henry Holt and Co., Inc., 1954), p. 165.

[6] Dora Greenwell, *Colloquia Crucis* (London: Strahan and Co., 1871), p. 15.

[7] Alan Paton, *Cry, the Beloved Country* (New York: Charles Scribner's Sons, 1951), p. 227.

[8] *Selected Letters of Baron Von Hugel,* edited by Bernard Holland (London: J. M. Dent & Sons, Ltd., 1928), p. 330.

CHAPTER 12

[1] Harry Emerson Fosdick, *What Is Vital in Religion* (New York: Harper & Row, Publishers, 1955), p. 218.

[2] Alfred Tennyson, "Ulysses," in *The Complete Poetical Works of Tennyson* (Boston: Houghton Mifflin Company, 1898), p. 88.

[3] John Oxenham, *A Saint in the Making* (London: Longmans, Green & Co. Ltd., 1931), p. 165.

[4] William Wordsworth, "To a Young Lady," in *The Complete Poetical Works of Wordsworth* (Boston: Houghton Mifflin Company, 1932), p. 327.

[5] Quoted in William Barclay, *Daily Celebration* (Waco: Word Books, 1971), p. 123.

[6] Luke Tyerman, *The Life and Times of John Wesley,* vol. 3 (London: Hodder and Stoughton Ltd., 1878), p. 629.

126 • COURAGE TO LIVE

[7] Victor Hugo quoted in "How Old Are You?" by David Christie, *British Weekly,* December 26, 1935.

[8] May Robson, quoted in *ibid.*

CHAPTER 13

[1] Leslie D. Weatherhead in *The City Temple Tidings,* September, 1959.

[2] *Letters of Thomas Erskine,* edited by William Hanna (Edinburgh: David Douglas, 1878), p. 205.

[3] Elizabeth Gray Vining, *Quiet Pilgrimage* (Philadelphia: J. B. Lippincott, 1970), p. 145.

[4] William Shakespeare, *Macbeth,* in *The Works of William Shakespeare* (New York: Oxford University Press, Inc., 1938), act 4, sc. 3, lines 114-115.

[5] Edmund Spenser, *The Faerie Queene,* Act II, Scene I, line 46.

[6] Harold Blake Walker, *To Conquer Loneliness* (New York: Harper & Row, Publishers, 1966), p. 142.

[7] *Ibid.*

CHAPTER 14

[1] Some portions of this chapter appeared as an Easter Sermon in *The Expository Times,* April, 1973, and this revised version is used by permission of the editor, Dr. C. L. Mitton, and the publishers, T. T. Clark of Edinburgh.

[2] Alex Munthe, *Story of San Michele* (New York: E. P. Dutton and Co., Inc., 1937), p. 505.

[4] Quoted in W. E. Sangster, *He Is Able* (London: Hodder and Stoughton Ltd., Stoughton Ltd., 1921), pp. 281-282.

[4] Quoted in W. E. Sangster, *He Is Able* (London: Hodder and Stoughton Ltd., 1933), p. 28.

[5] Quoted in *Sangster at Filey* (Croydon: New Mildmay Press, 1961), p. 54.

[6] John Donne, "Death Be Not Proud" in *The Complete Poems of John Donne,* ed. Roger E. Bennett (Chicago: Packard and Company, 1942), p. 269.

[7] Joseph H. Oldham, *Florence Allshorn and The Story of St. Julian's* (New York: Harper & Row, Publishers, n.d.), p. 162.

[8] Richard Collier, *Booth: The General Next to God* (London: Allen, 1965), p. 245.

[9] Editor's Foreword in Dietrich Bonhoeffer, *Letters and Papers from Prison,* trans. Reginald H. Fuller (New York: The Macmillan Company, 1953), p. 14.

[10] From "When Life Is the Climax of Death" by Morris Wee in Alton M. Motter, ed., *Preaching the Resurrection* (Philadelphia: Fortress Press, 1959), p. 186. Reprinted with the permission of the publisher.